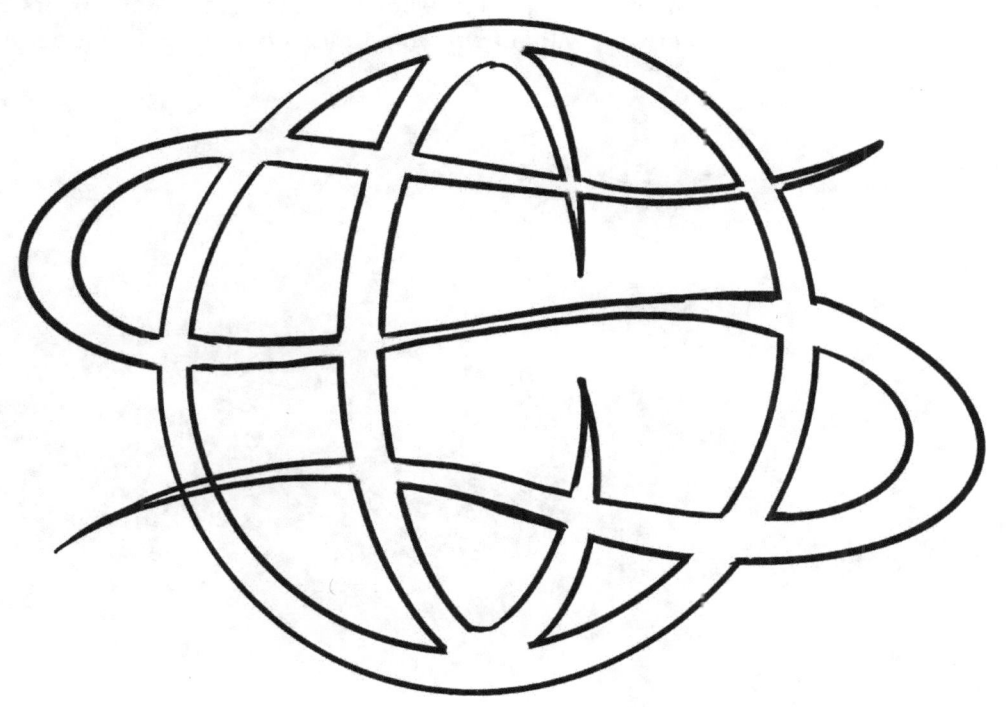

No part of this publication may be reproduced, stored in a retrieval system,
Or transmitted in any form or by any means, electronic, mechanical, photocopying,
Recording, or otherwise, without written permission of the publisher.

COPYRIGHT 2002 JOHN SPANGLER
https://jspangler20.wixsite.com/mysite
https://www.facebook.com/jspangler20
spanglerscreations@yahoo.com
Instagram: john_spanglerscreations

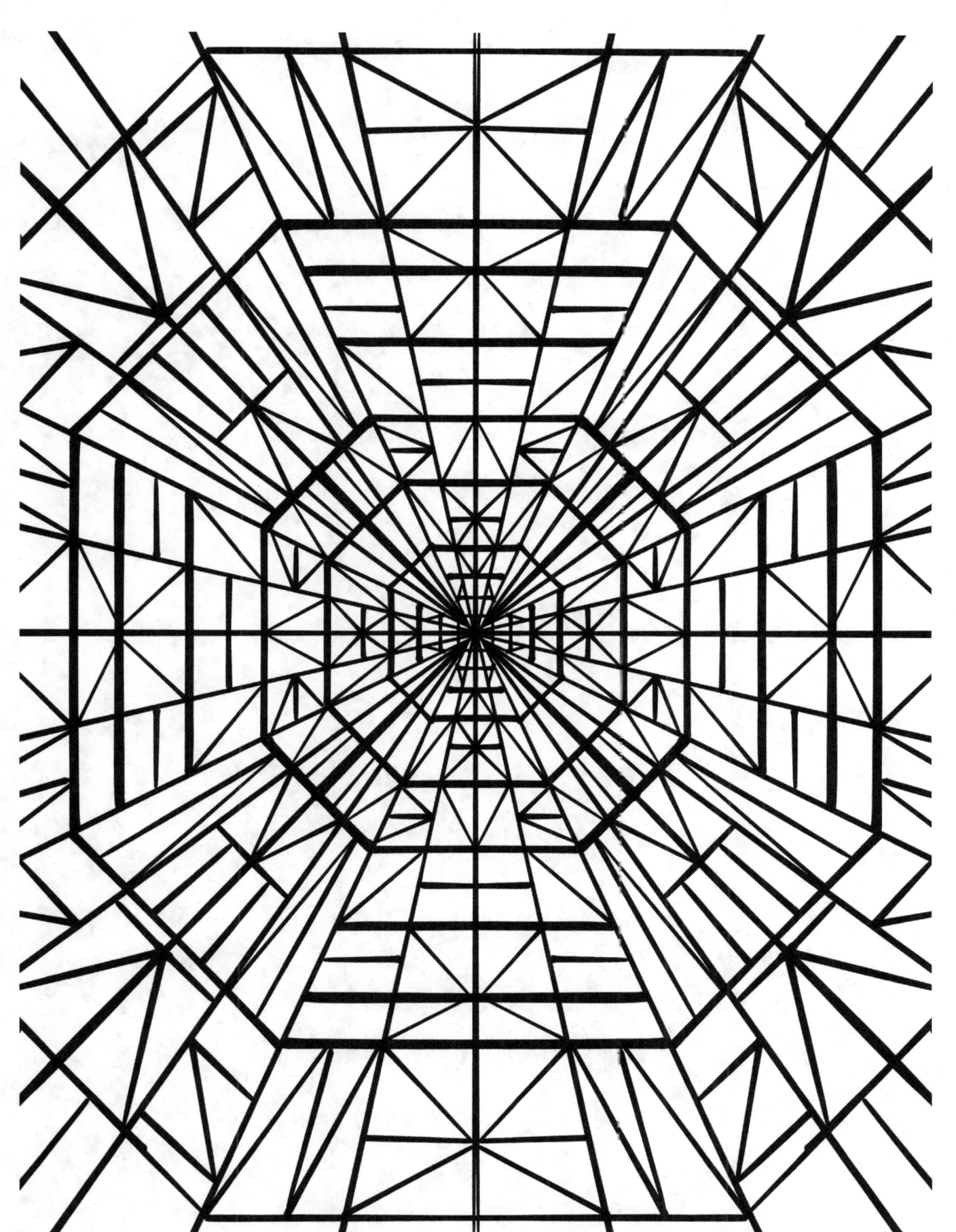

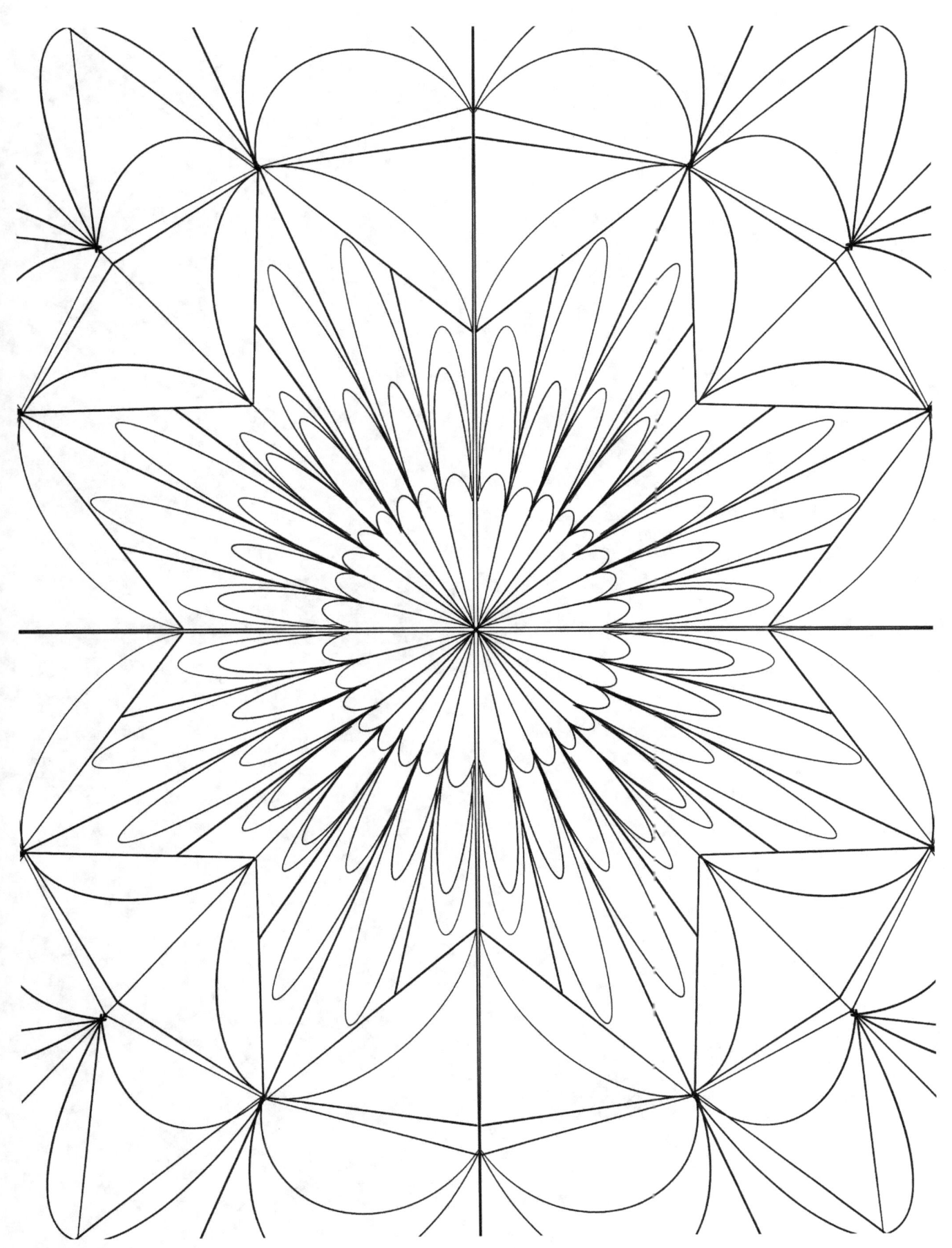

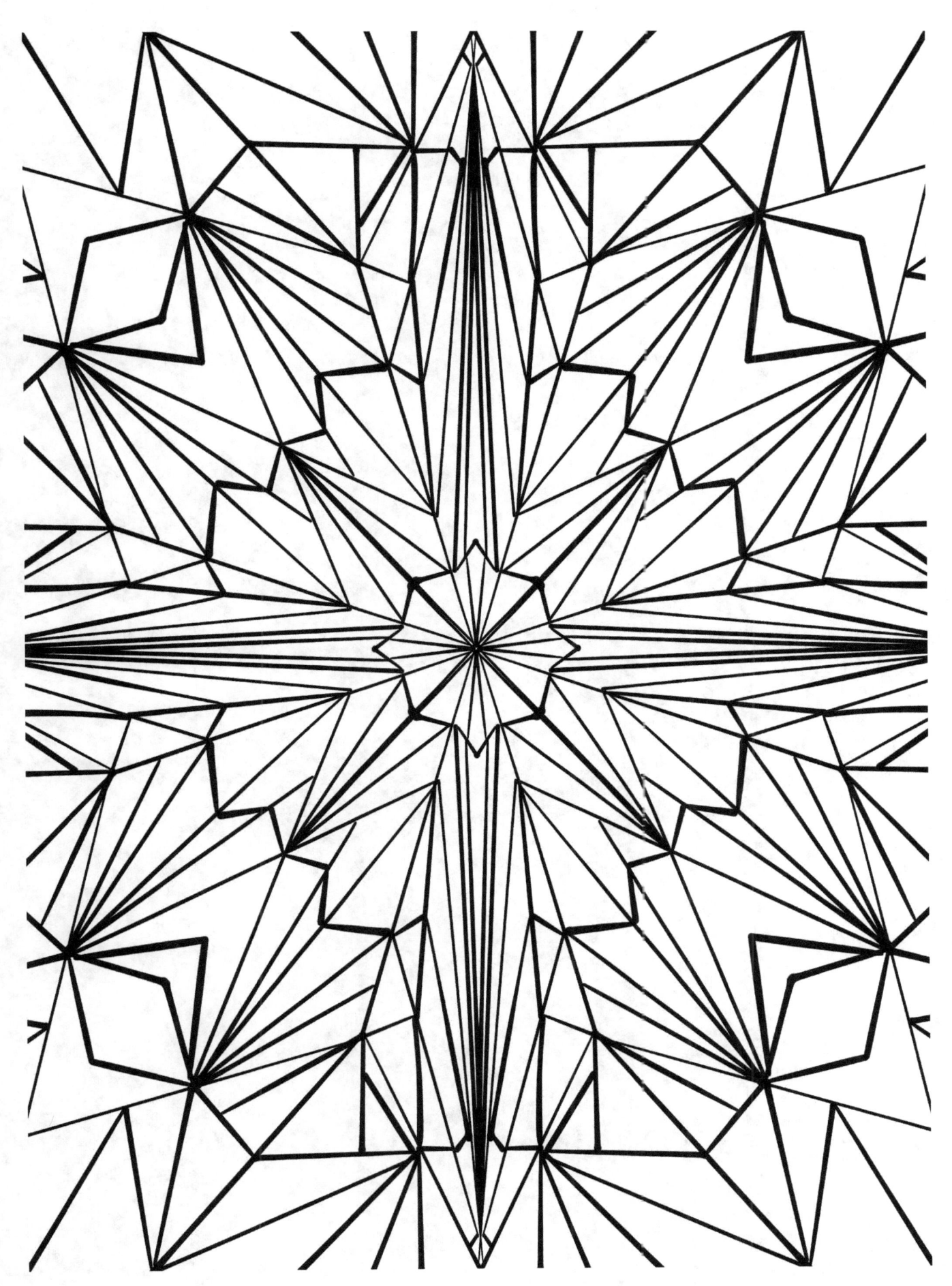

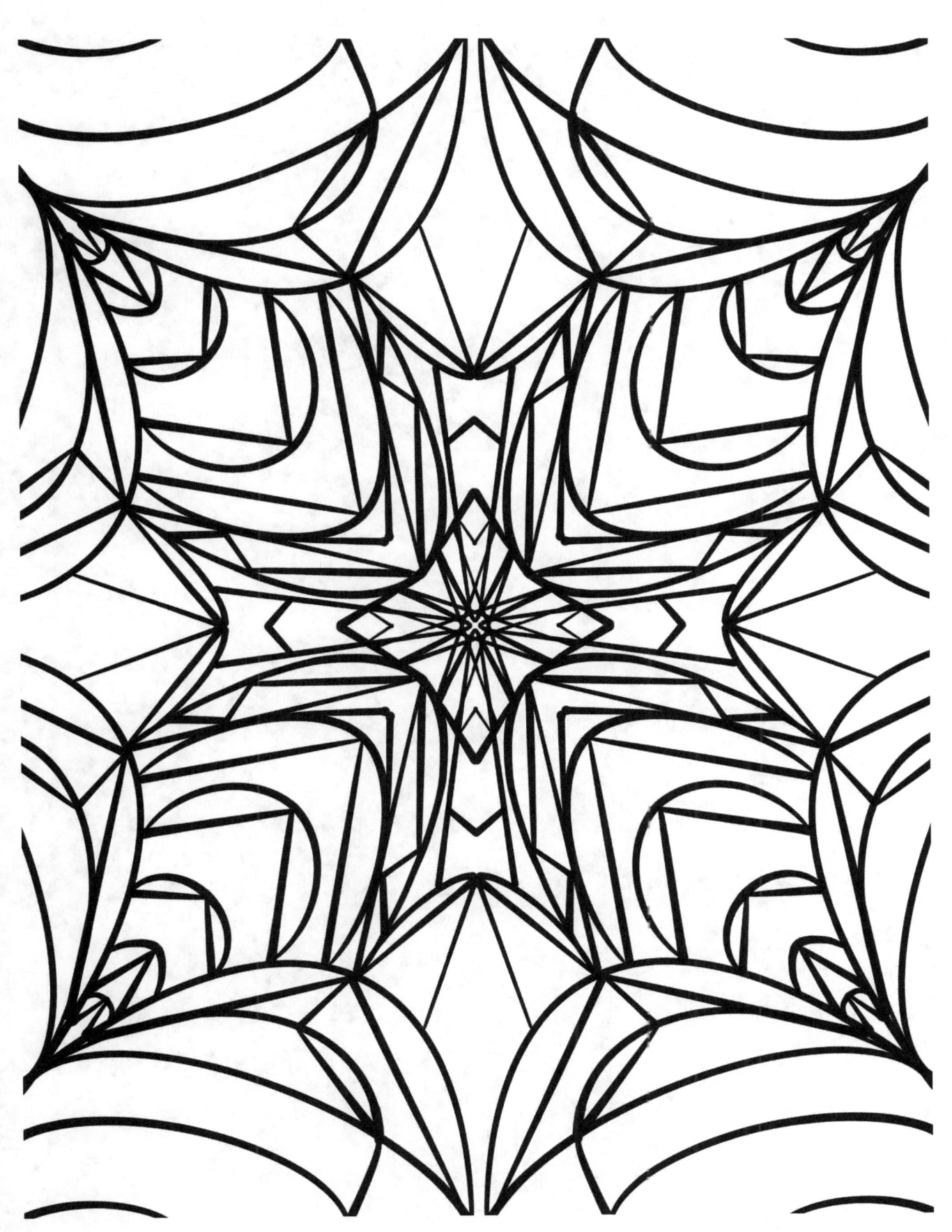

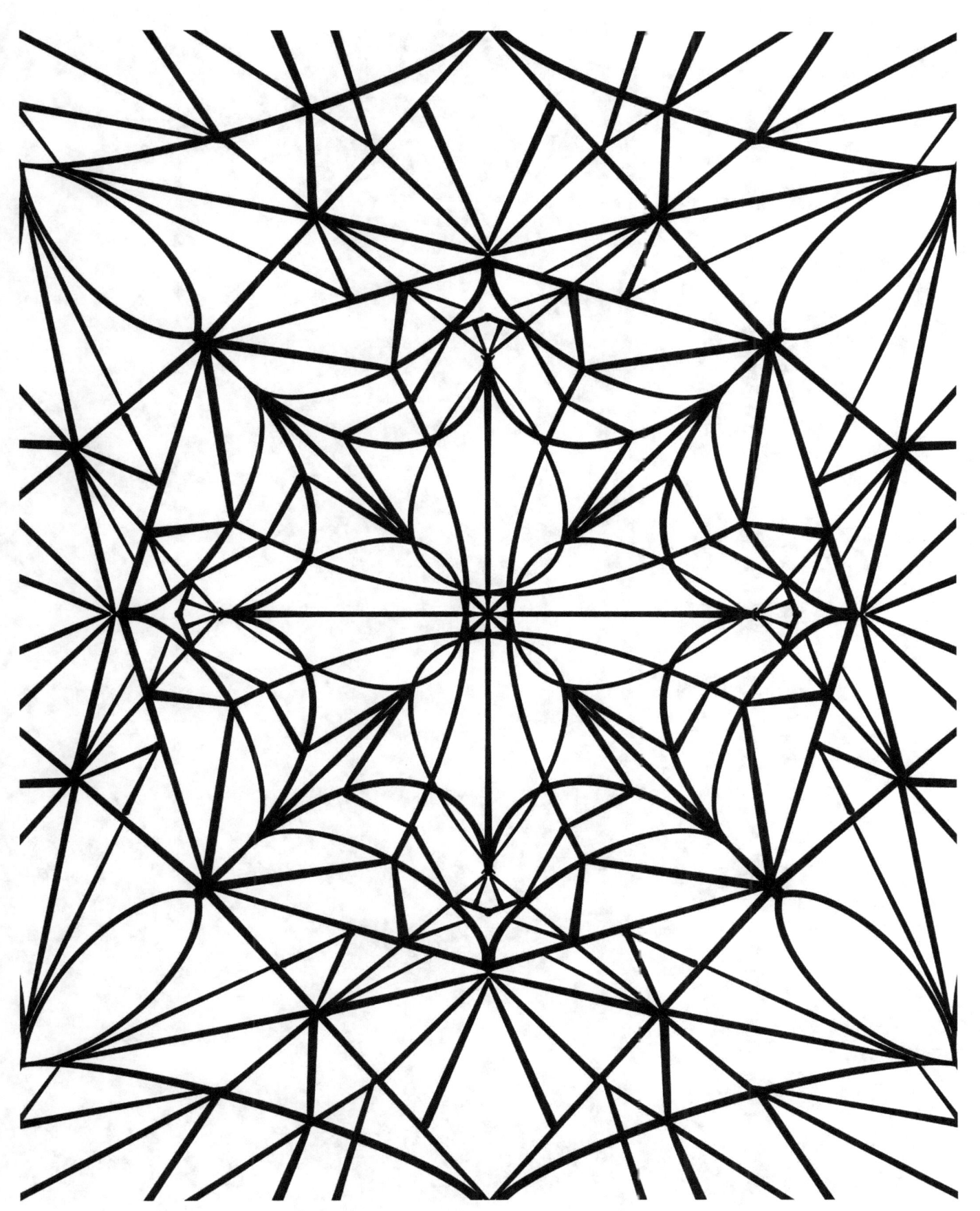

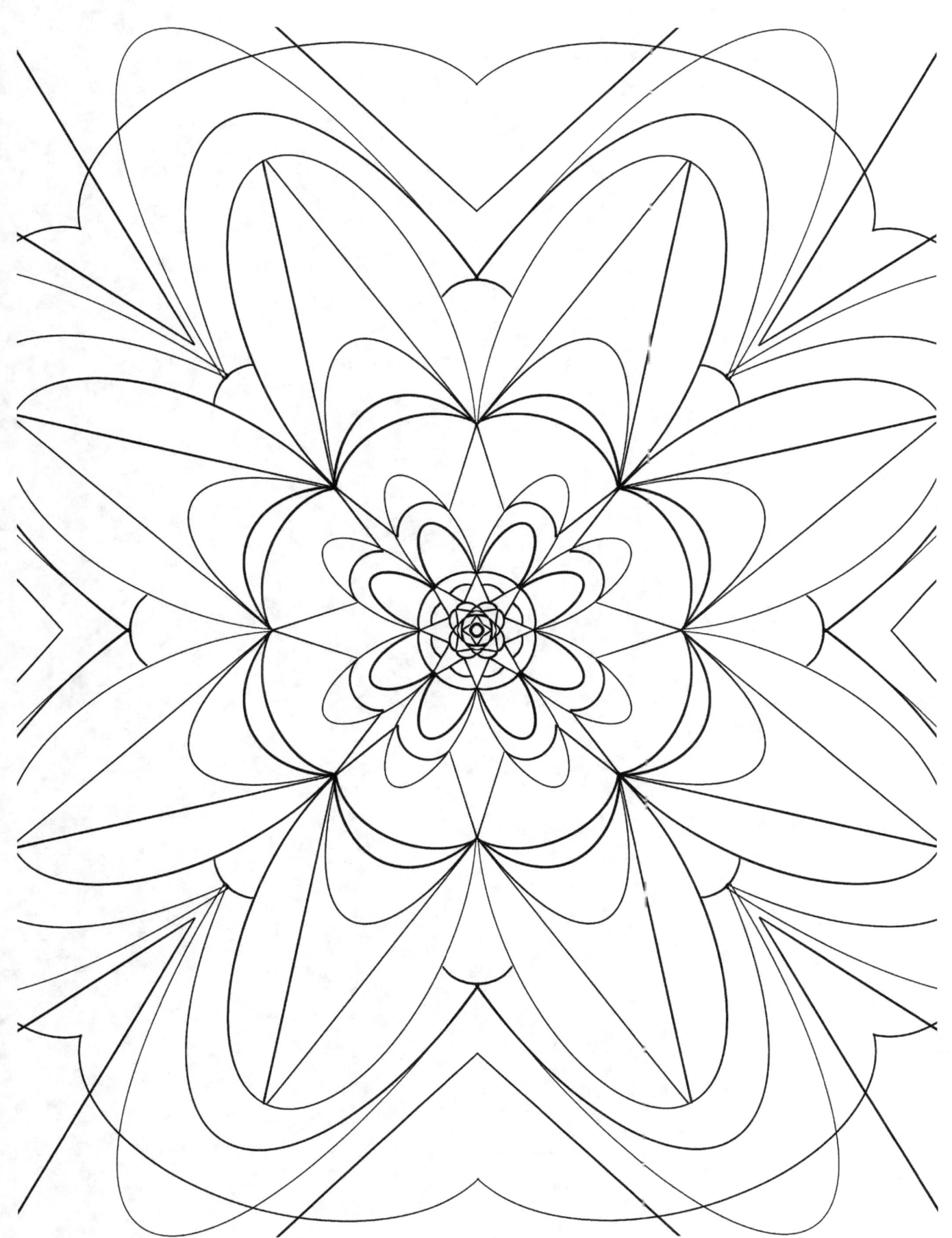

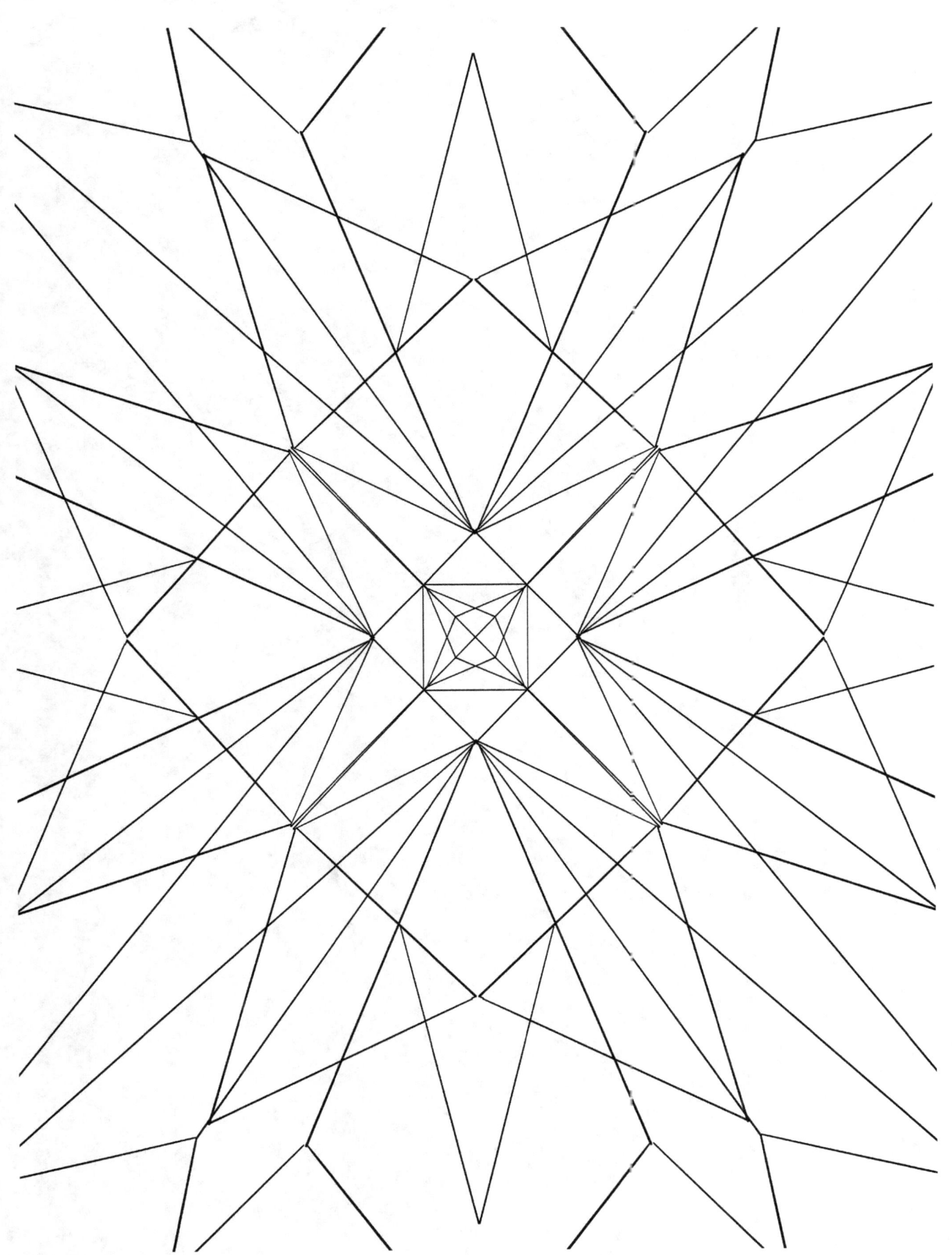

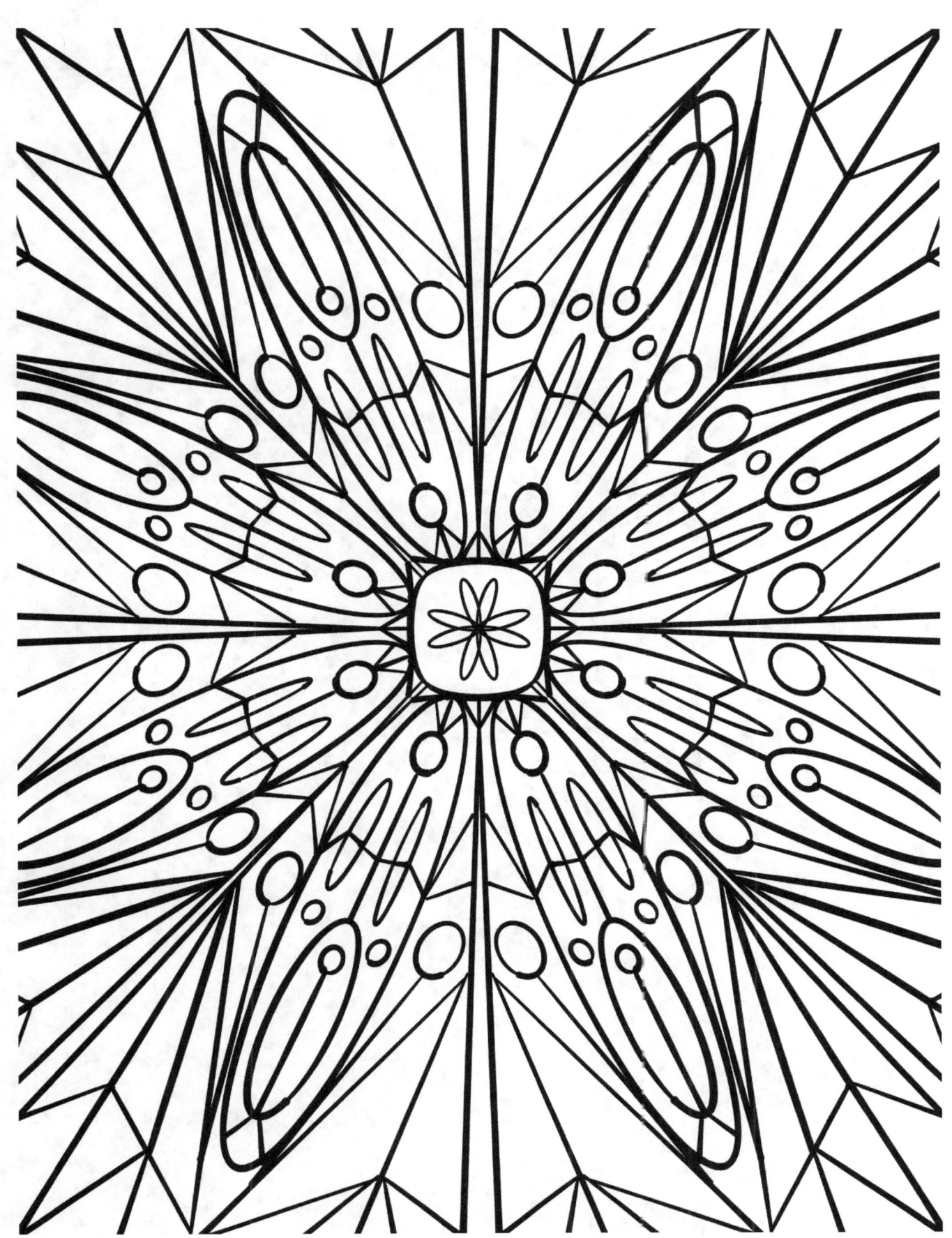

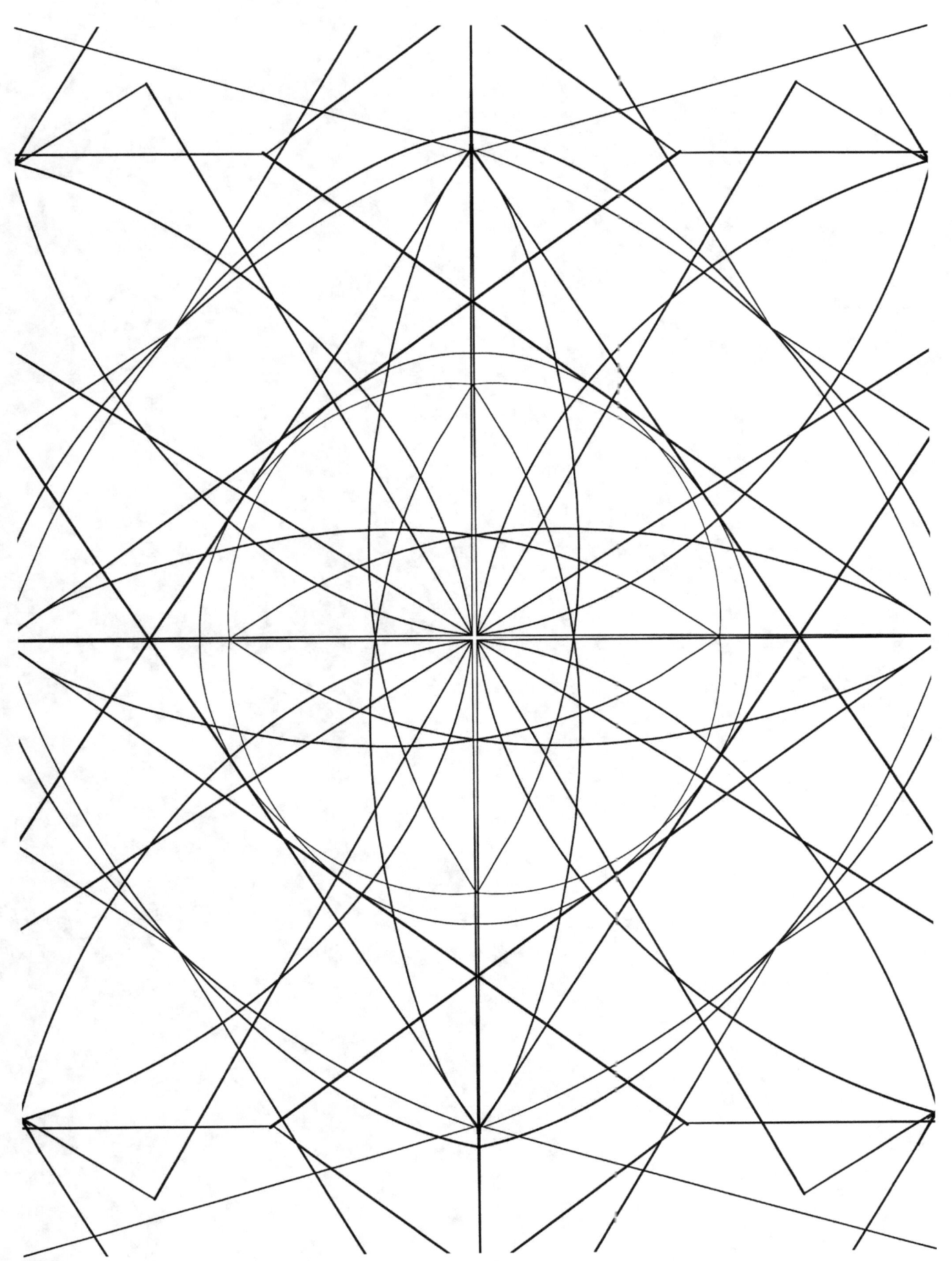

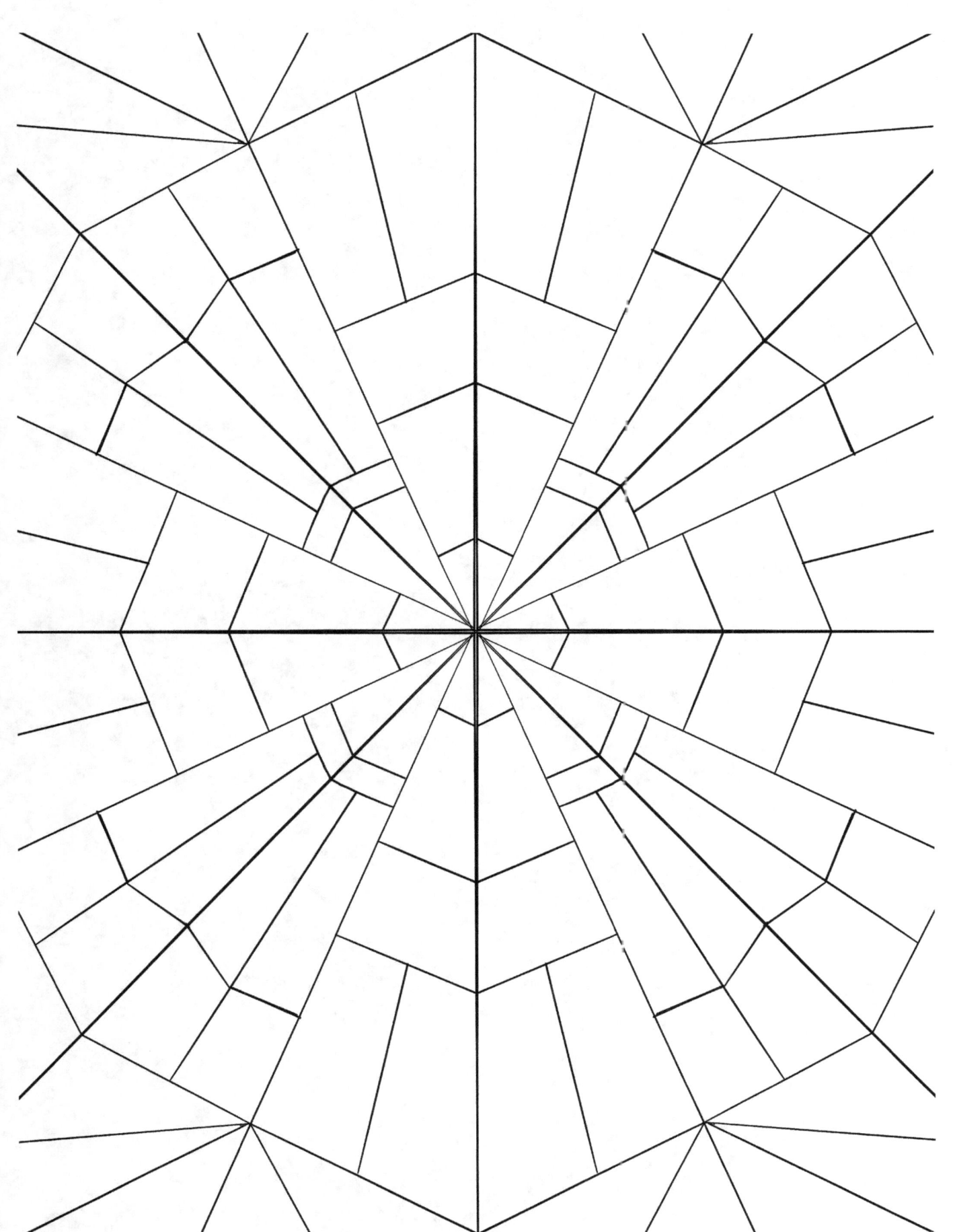

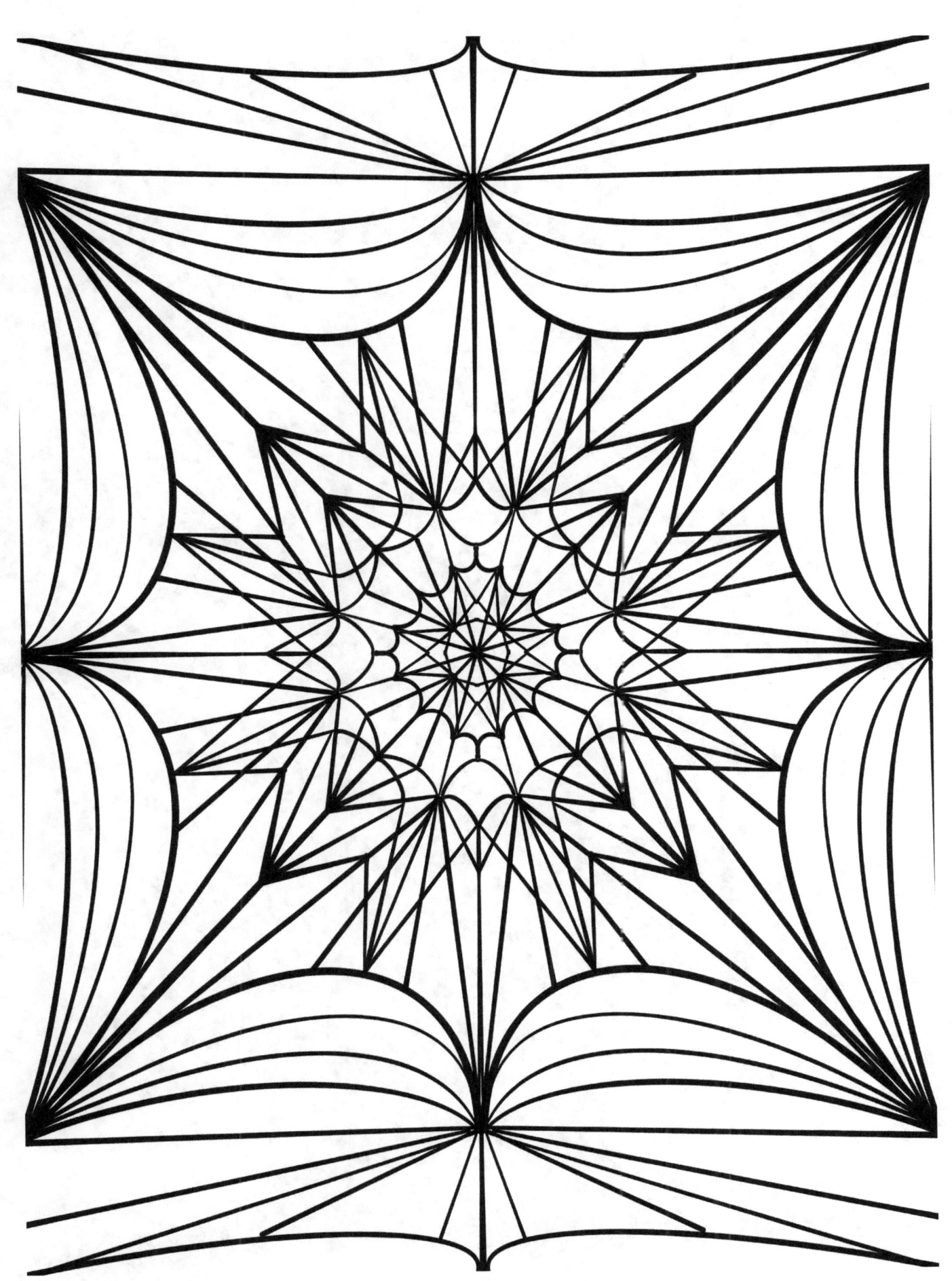

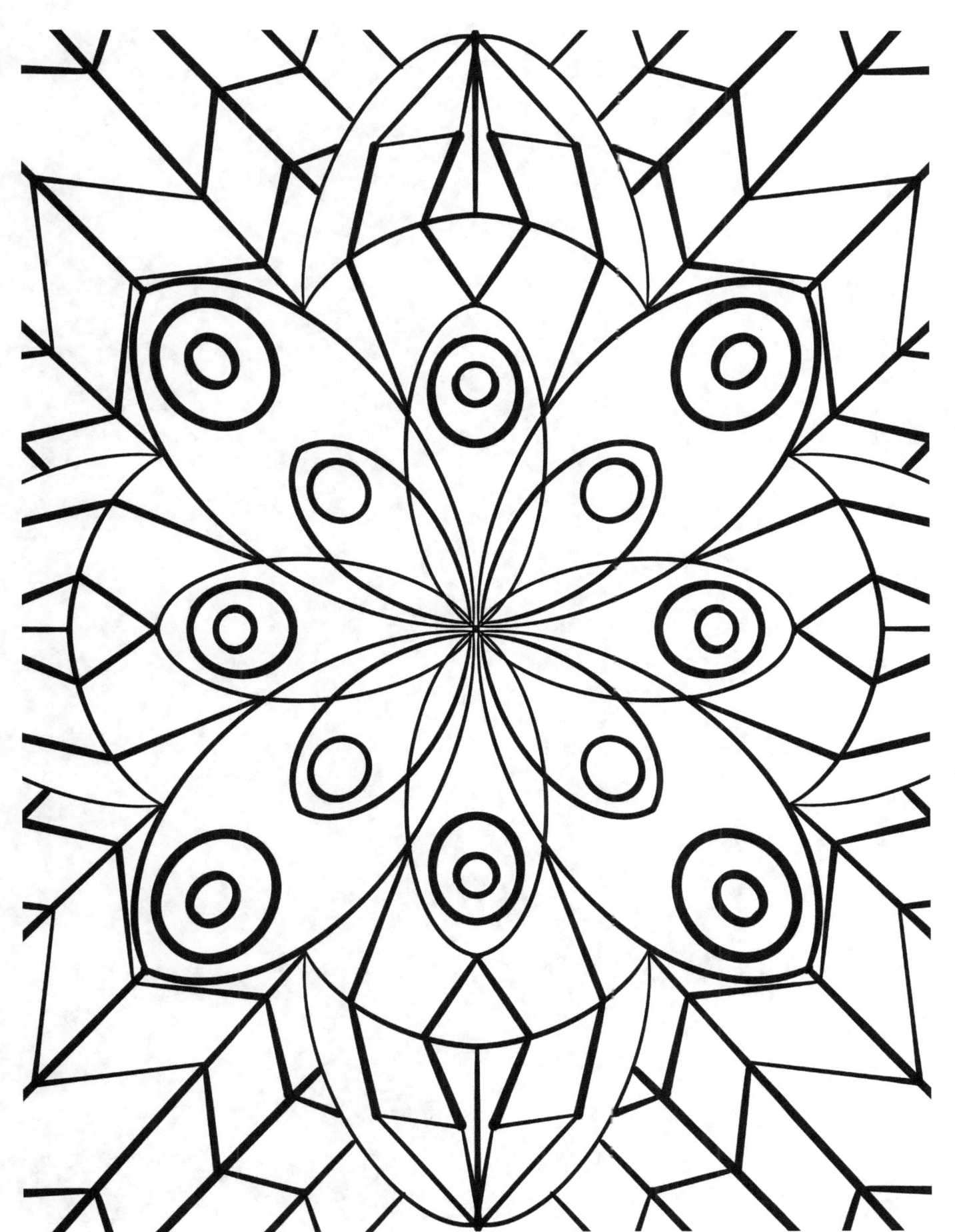

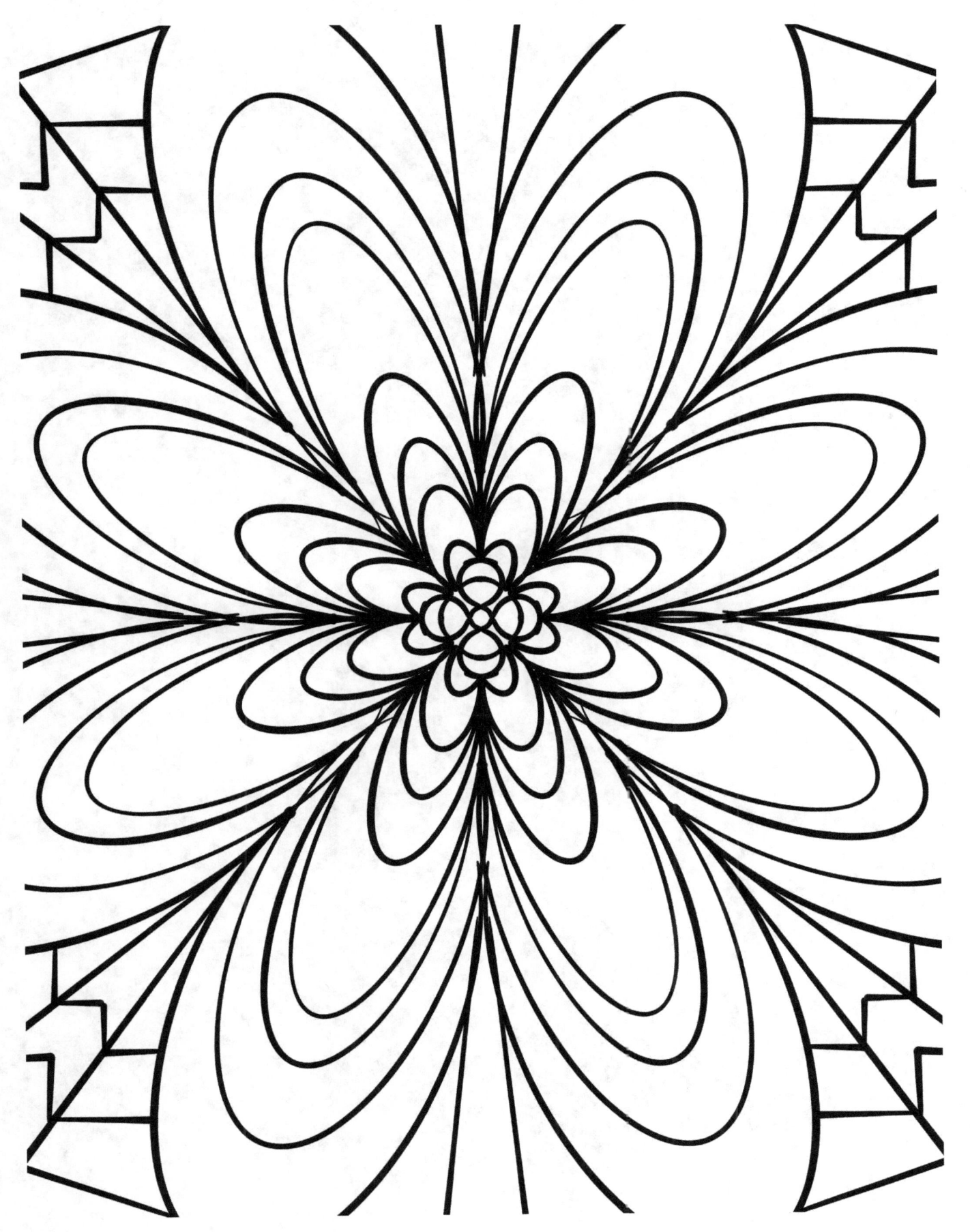

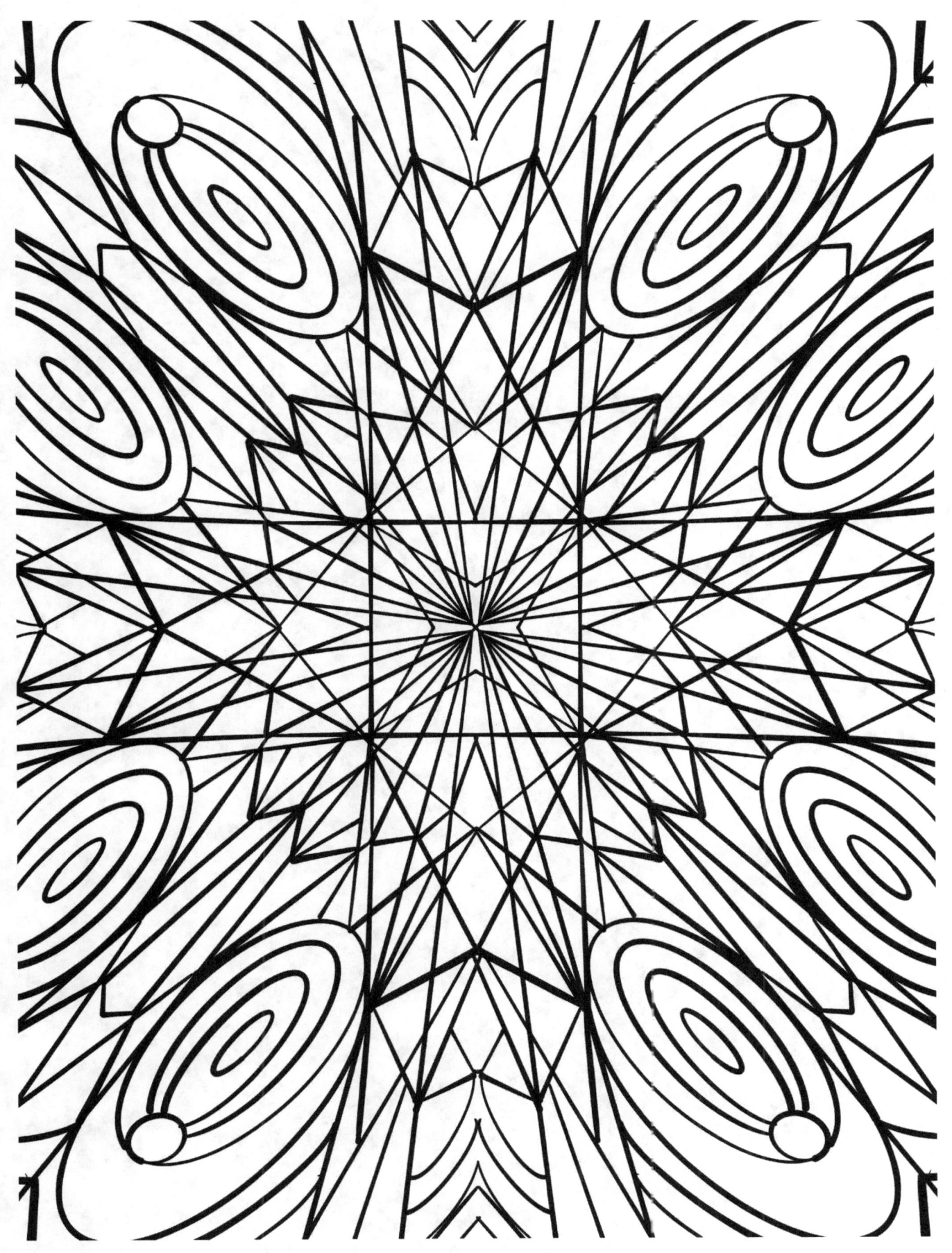

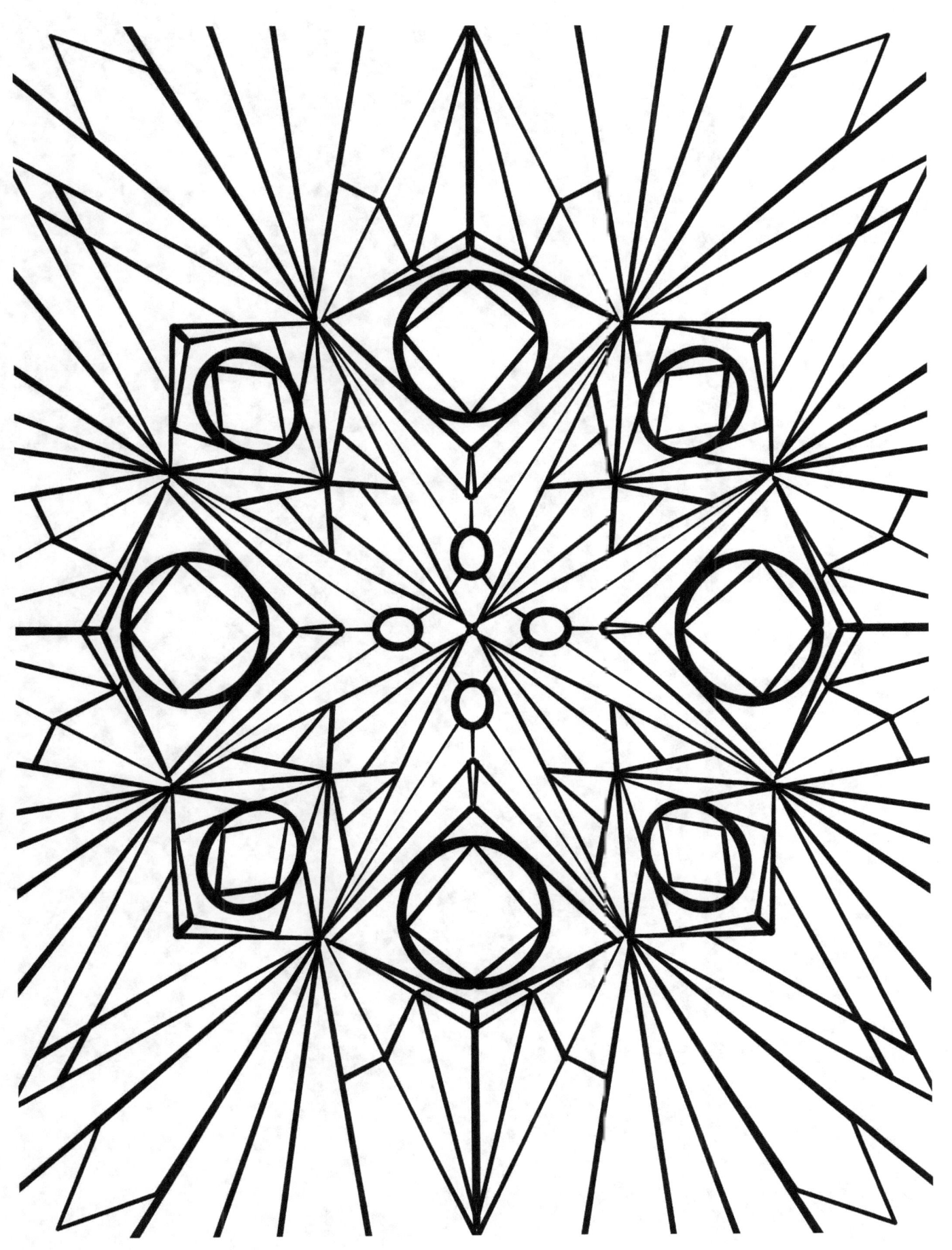

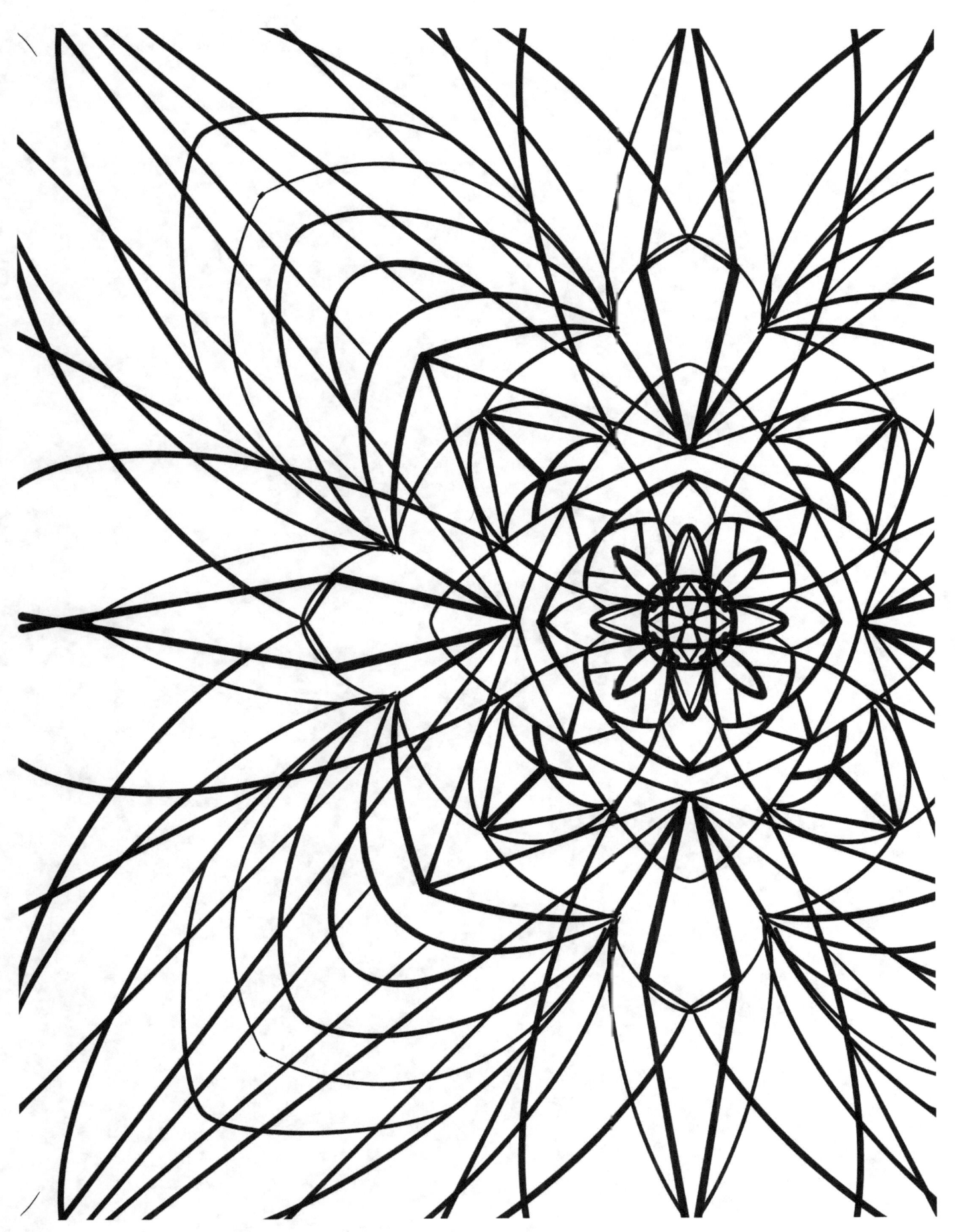

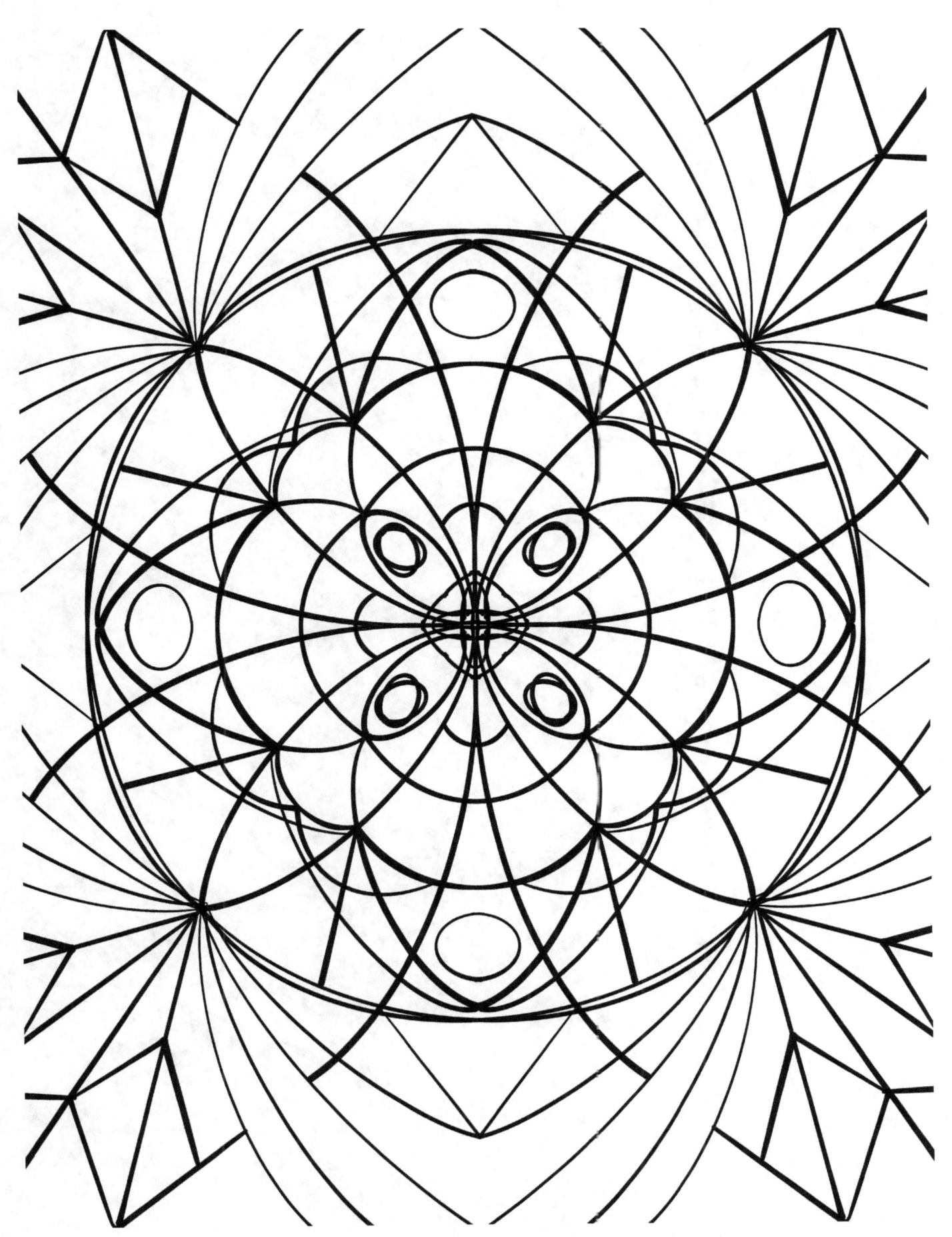

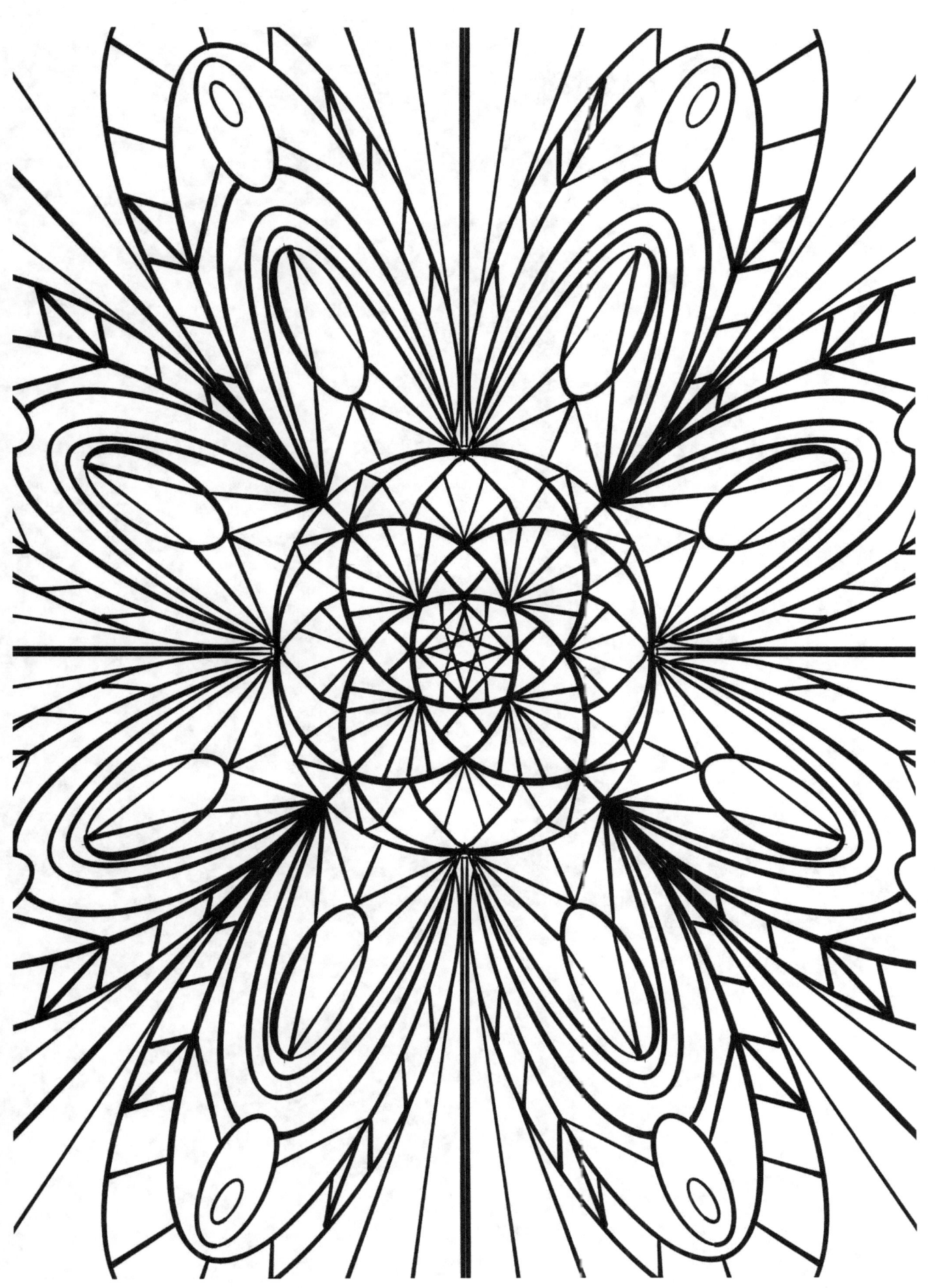

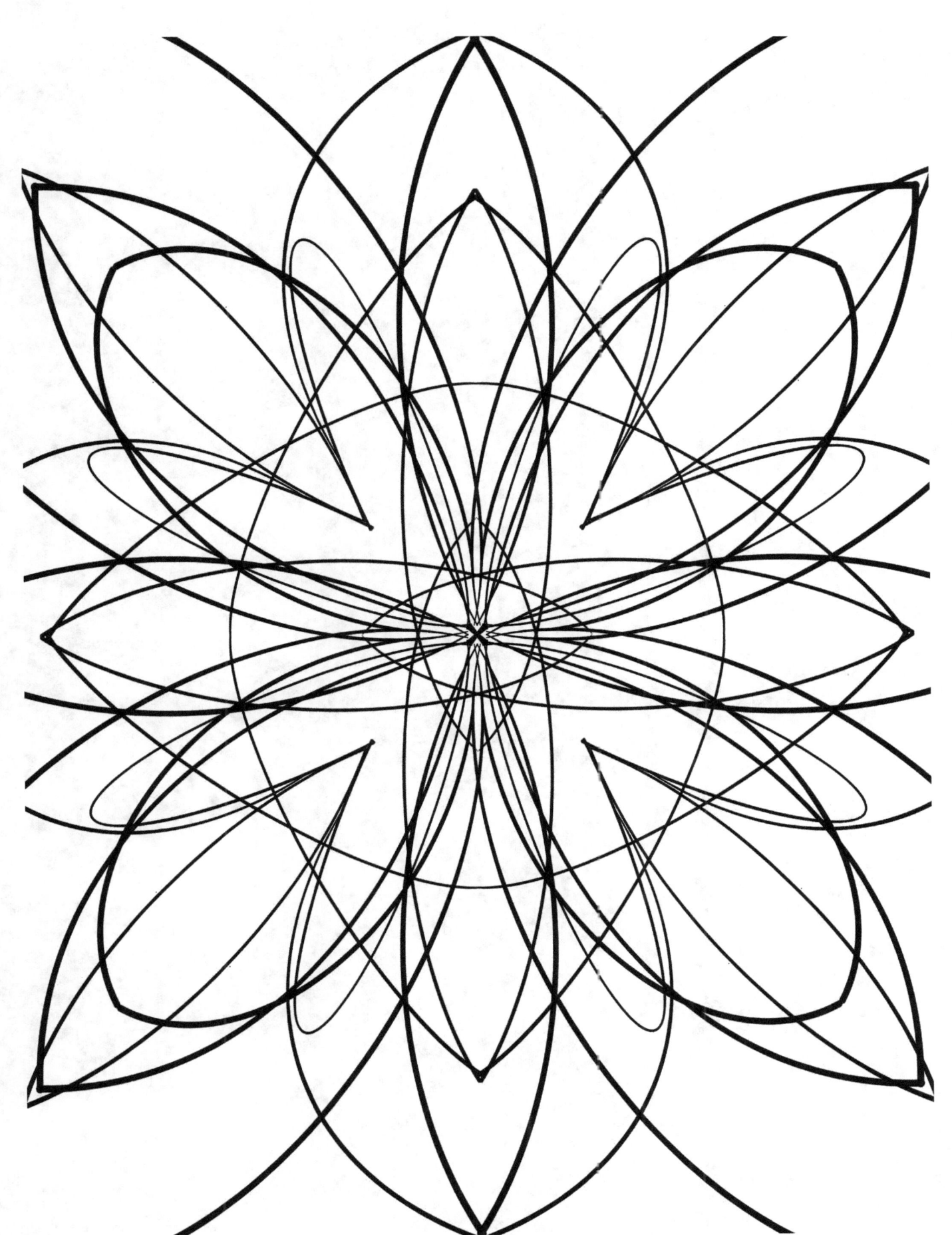

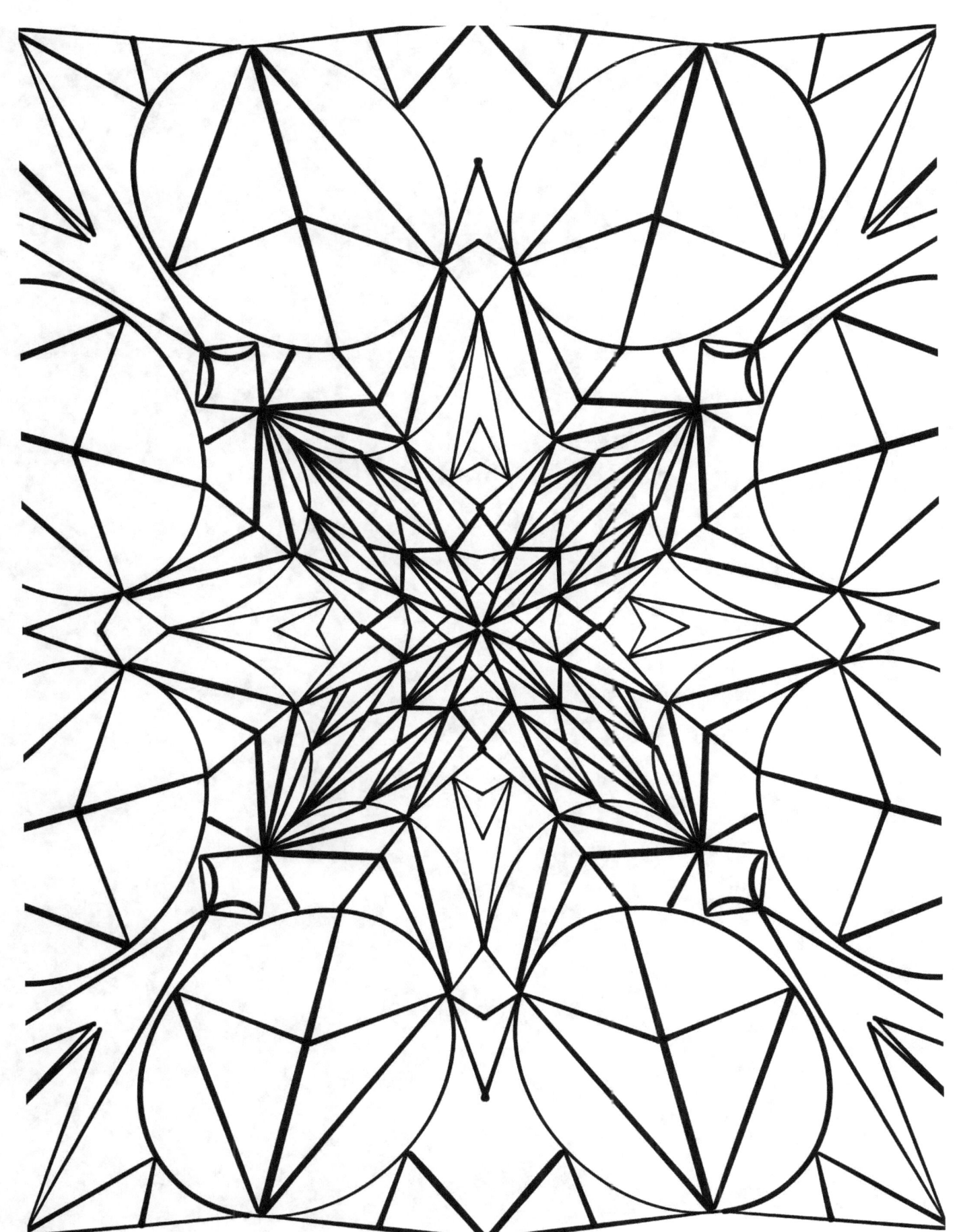

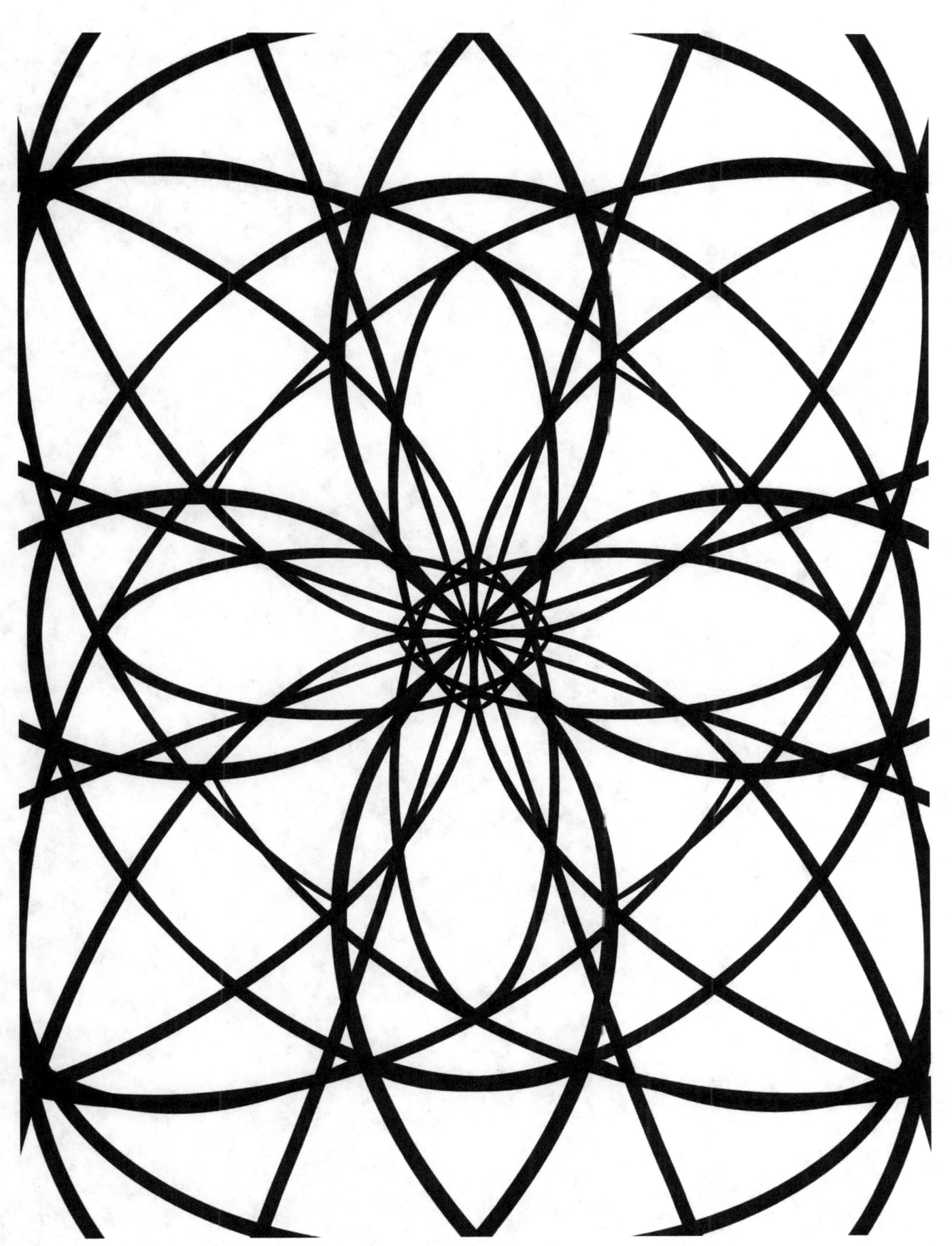

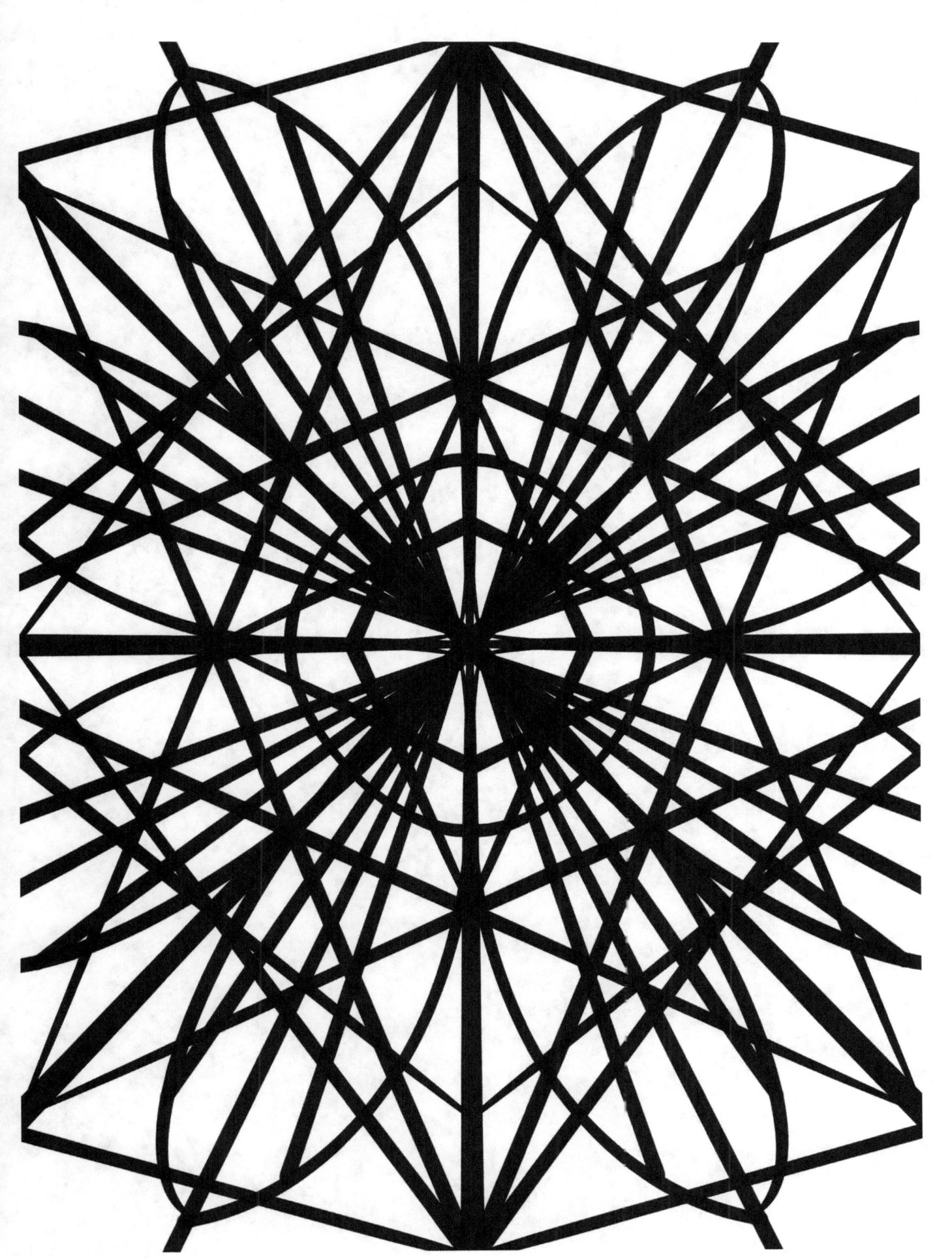

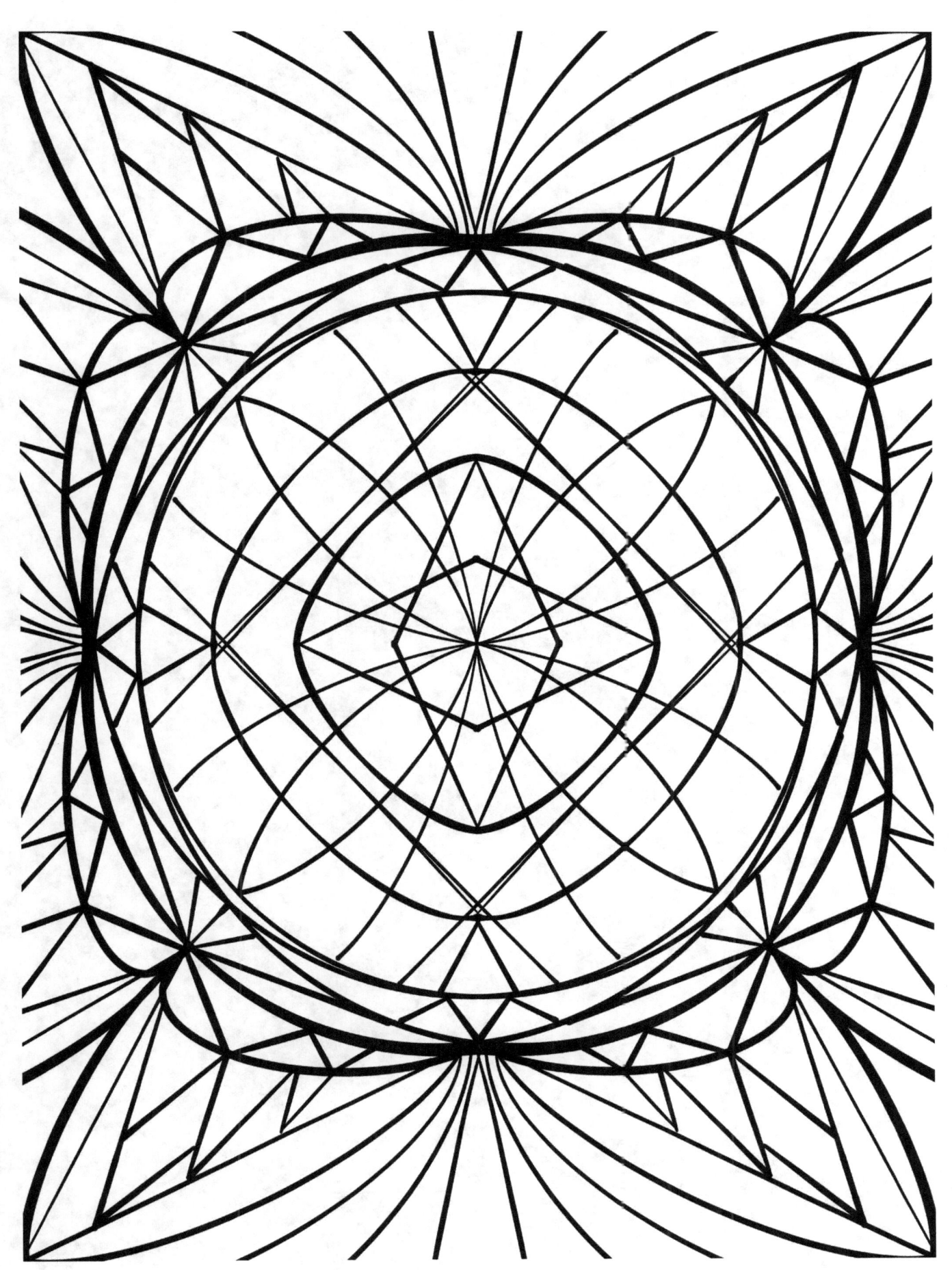

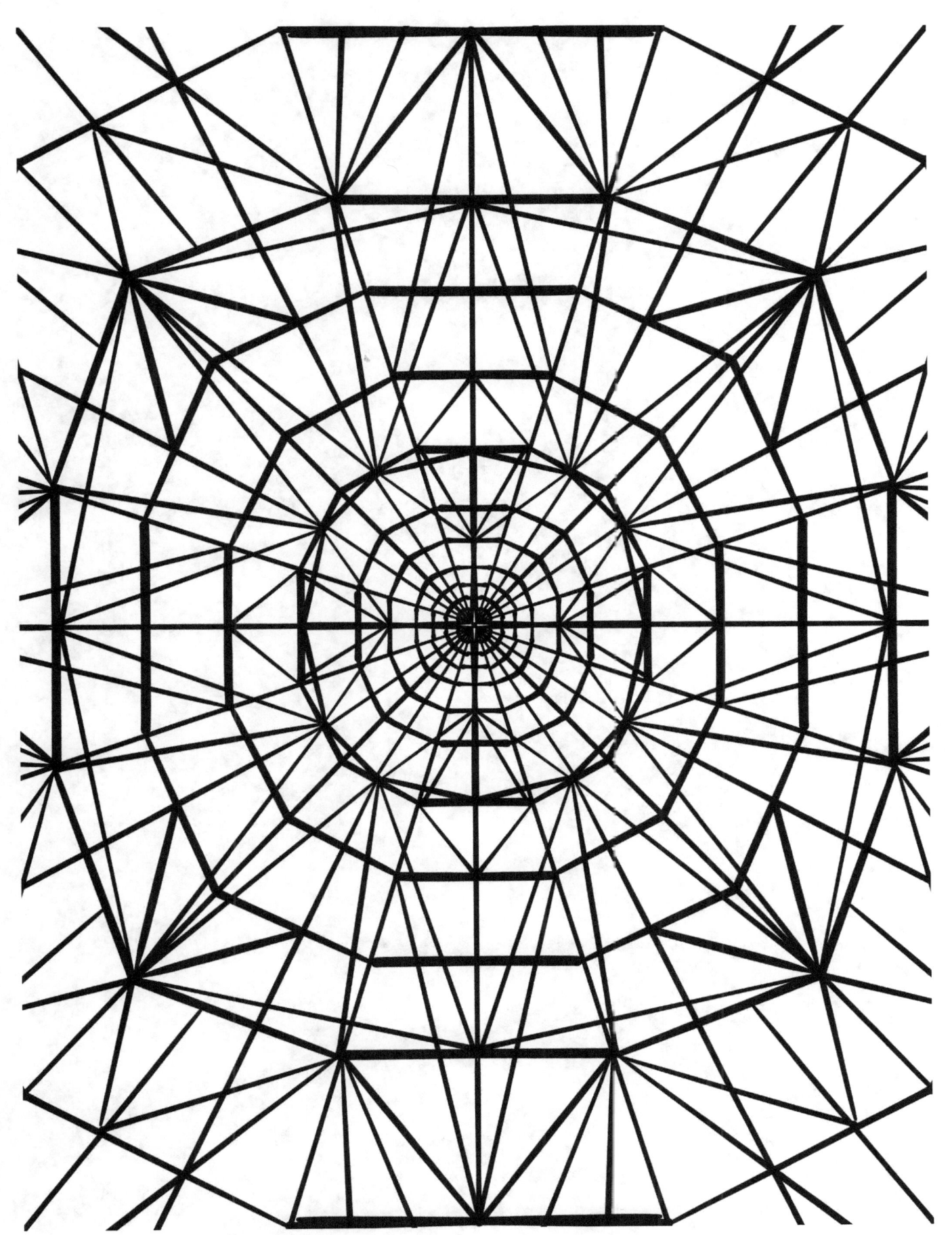

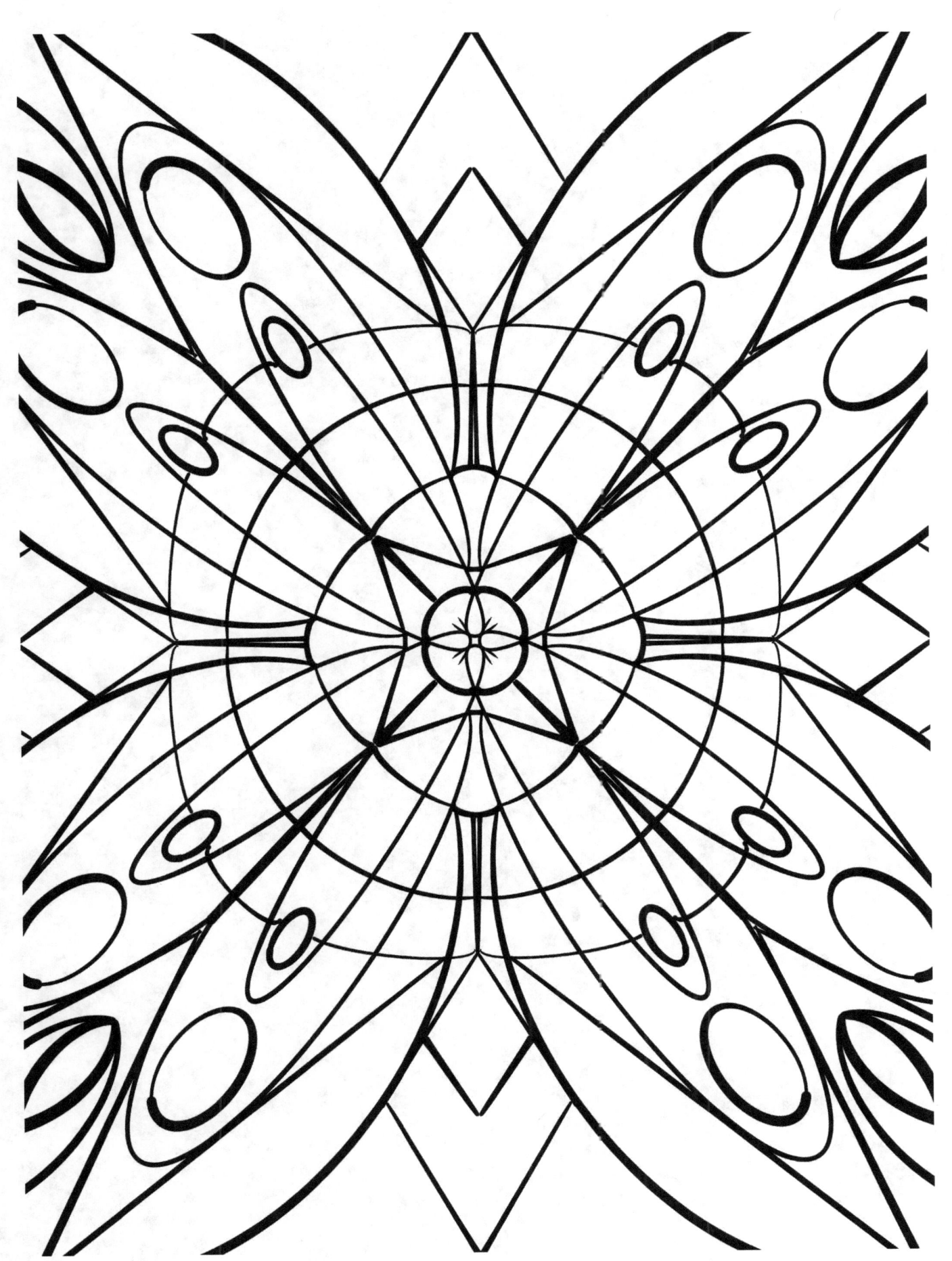

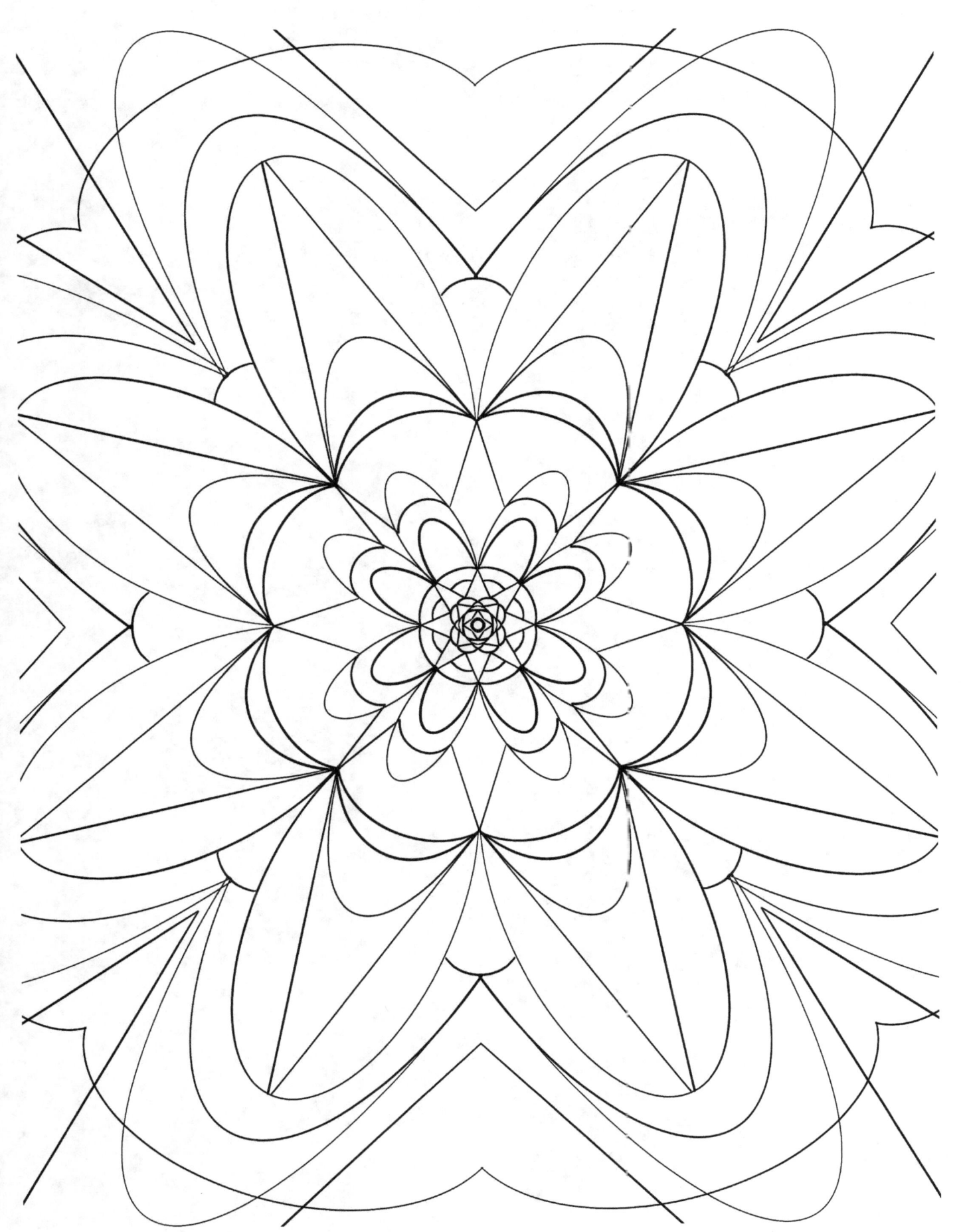

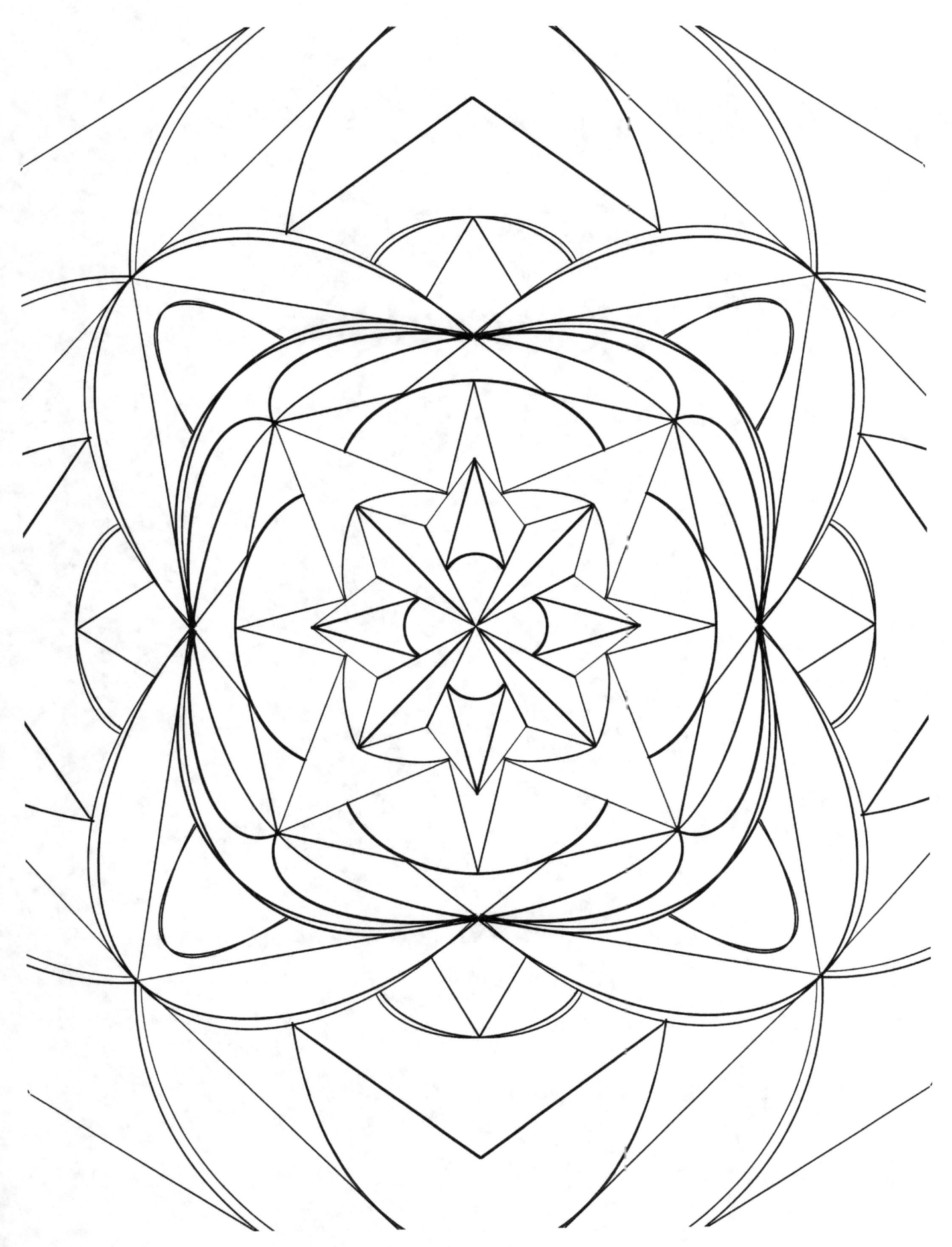

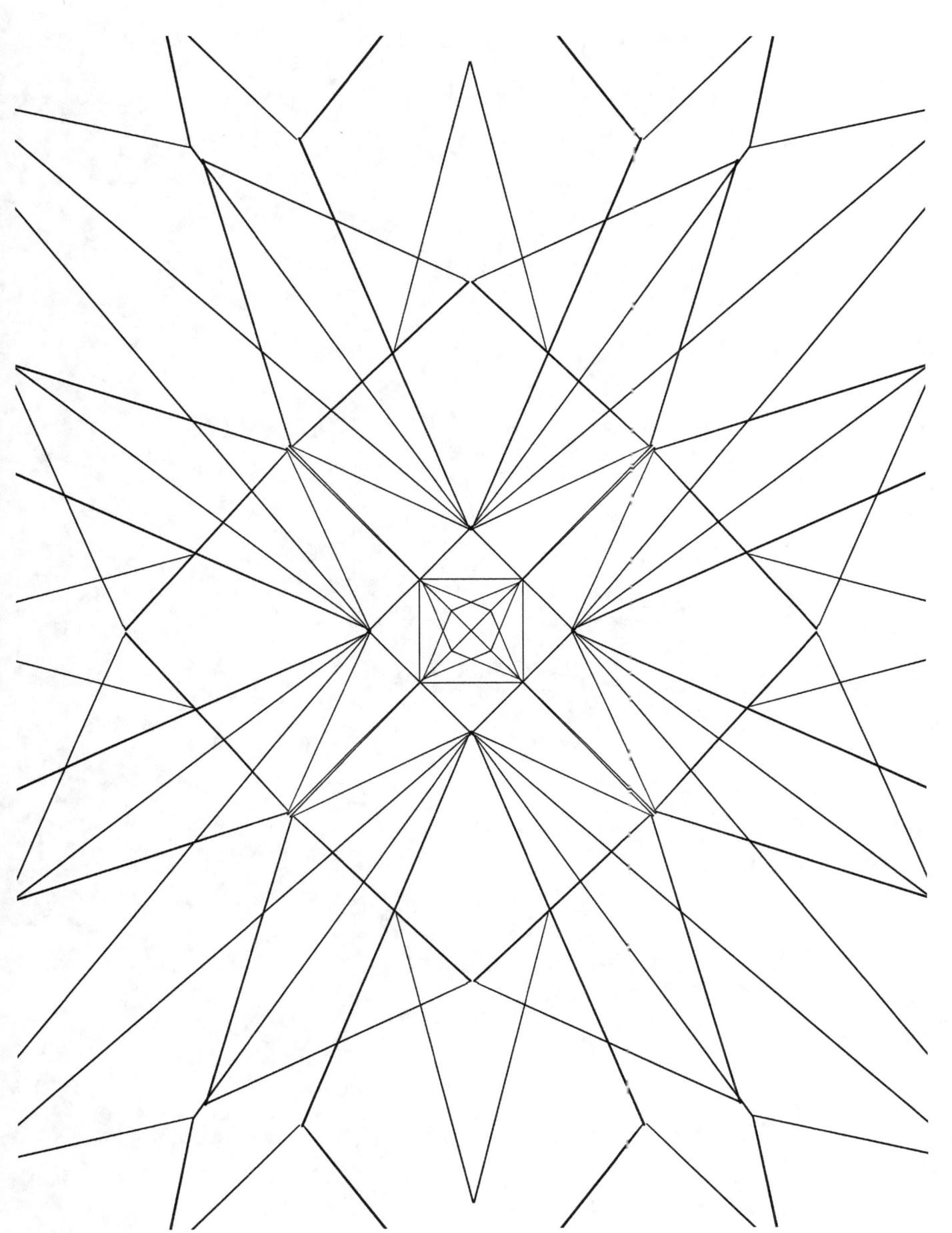

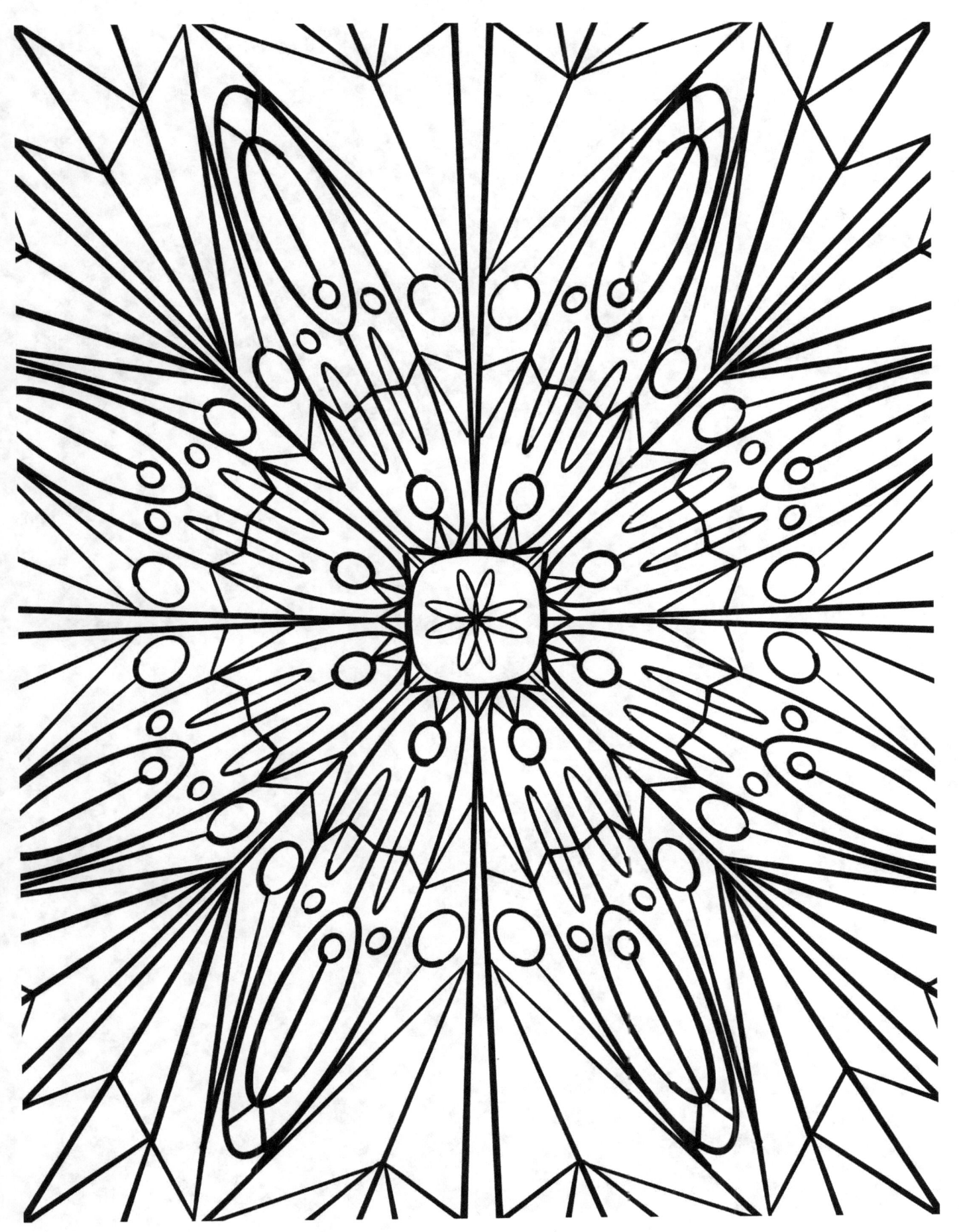

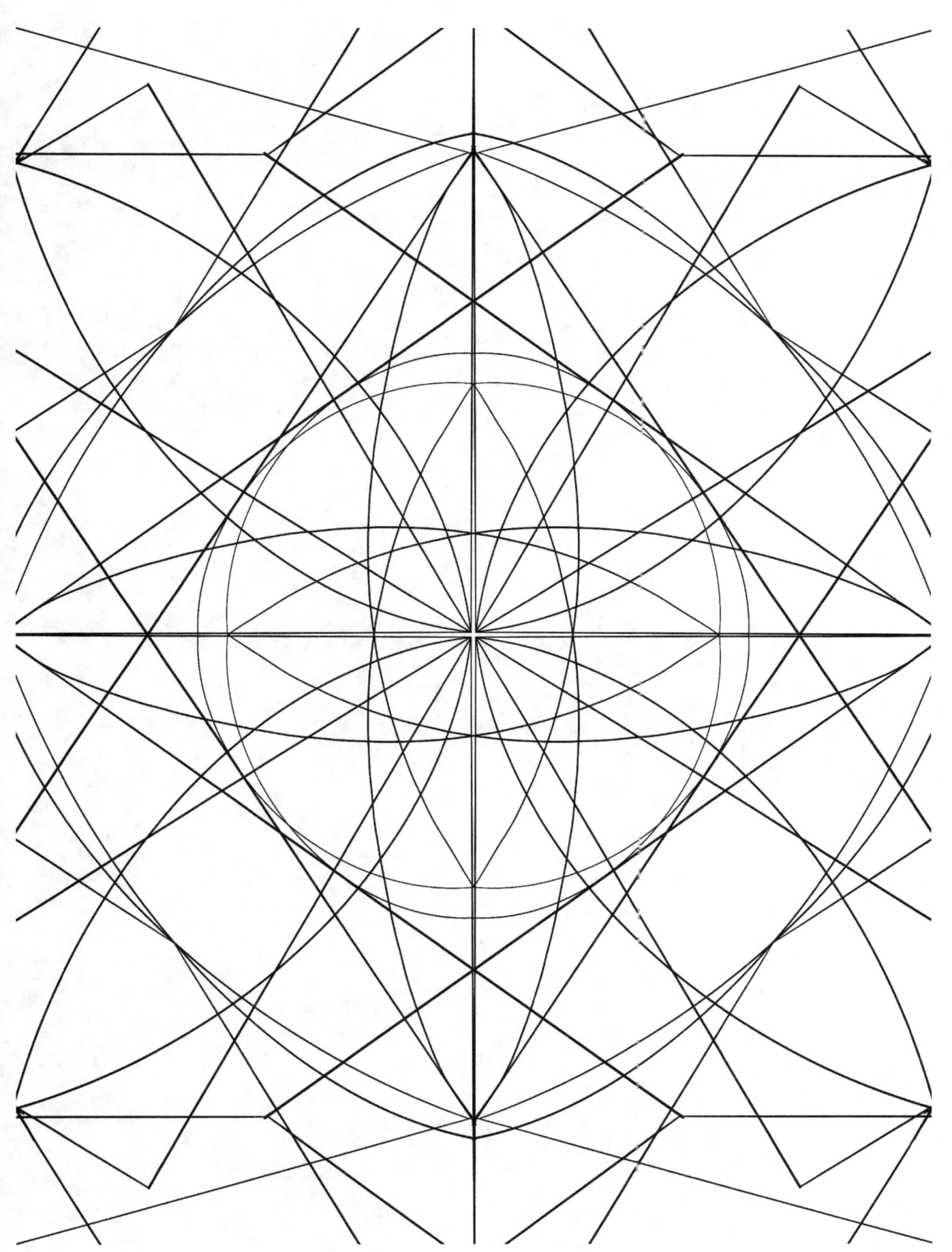

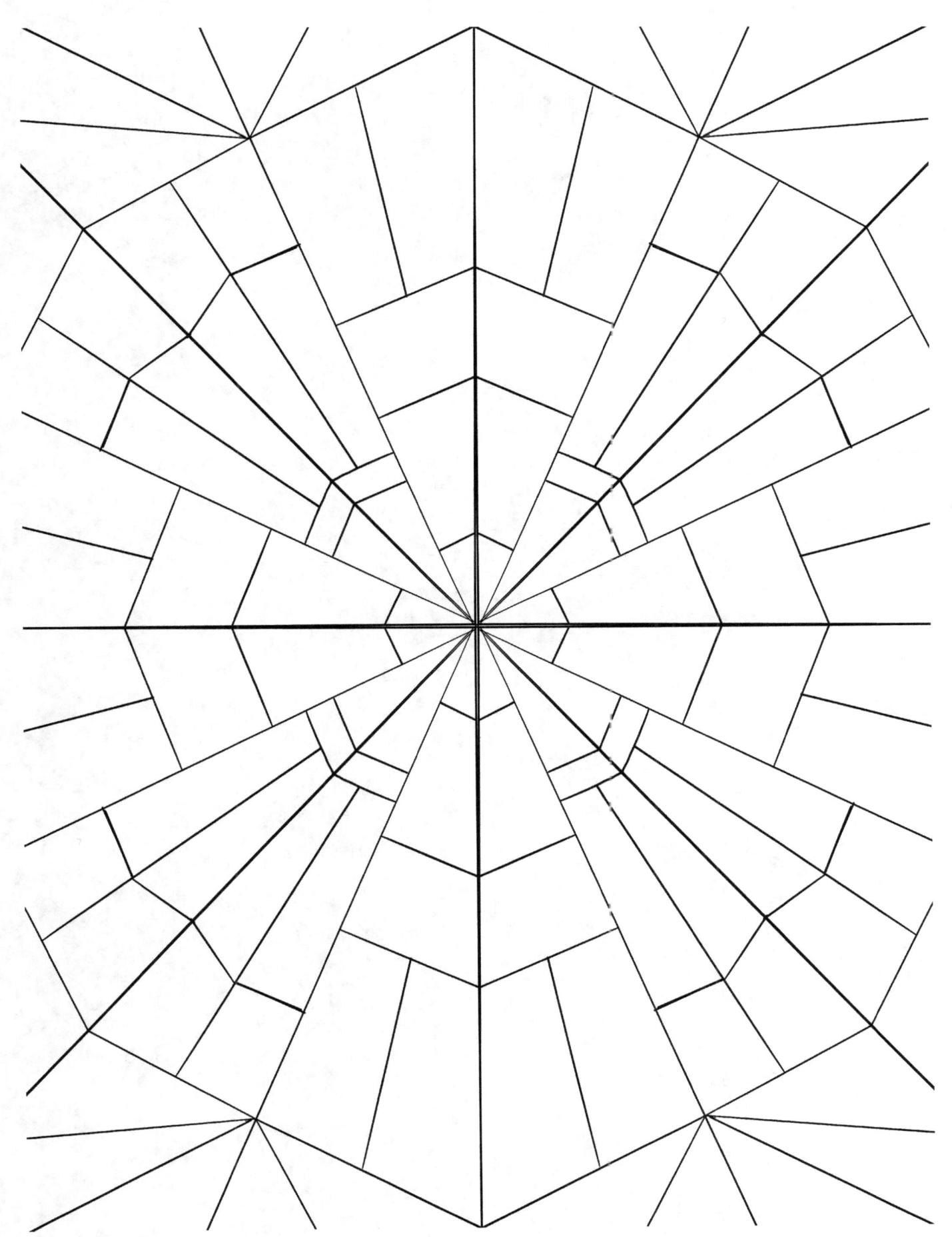

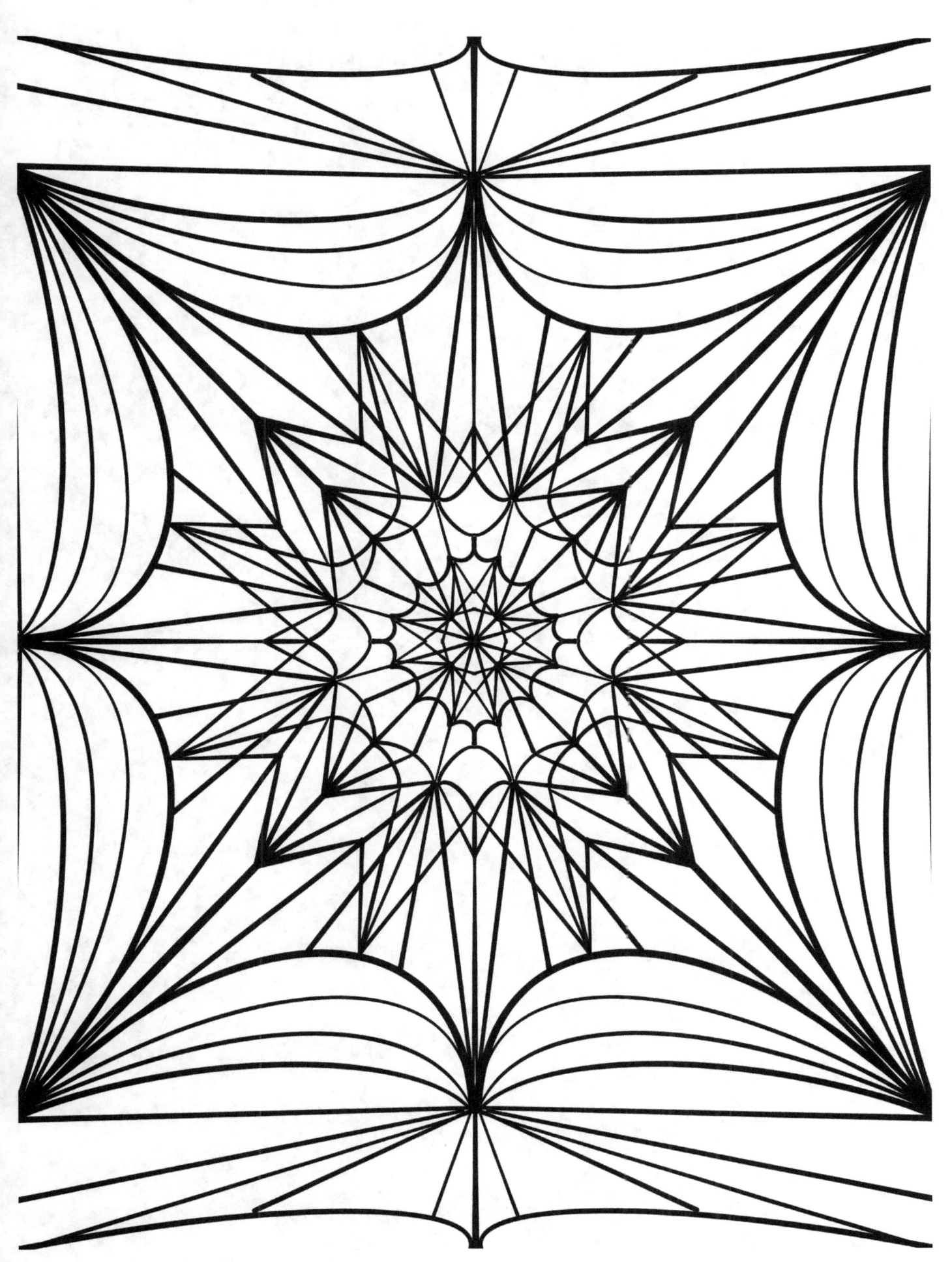

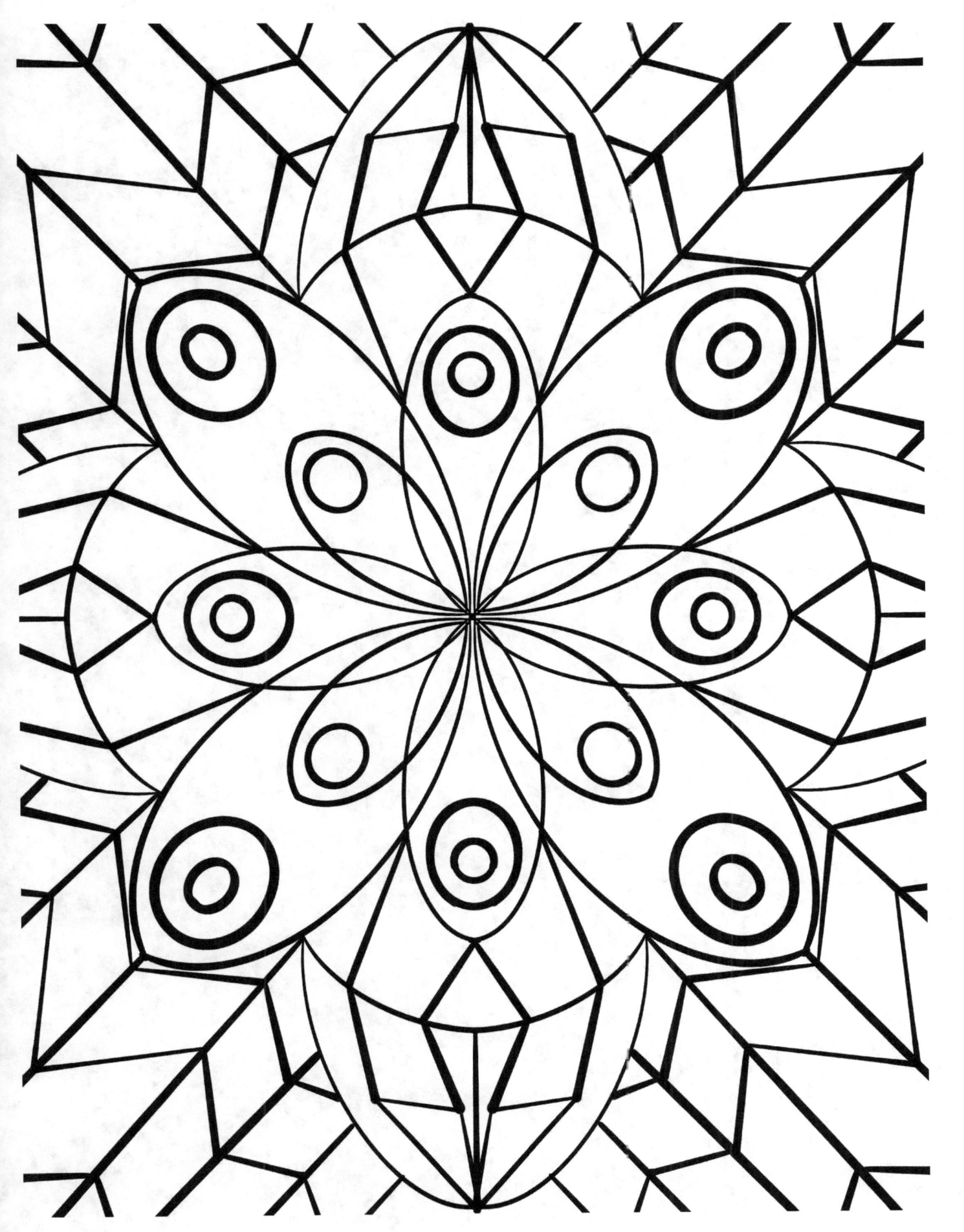

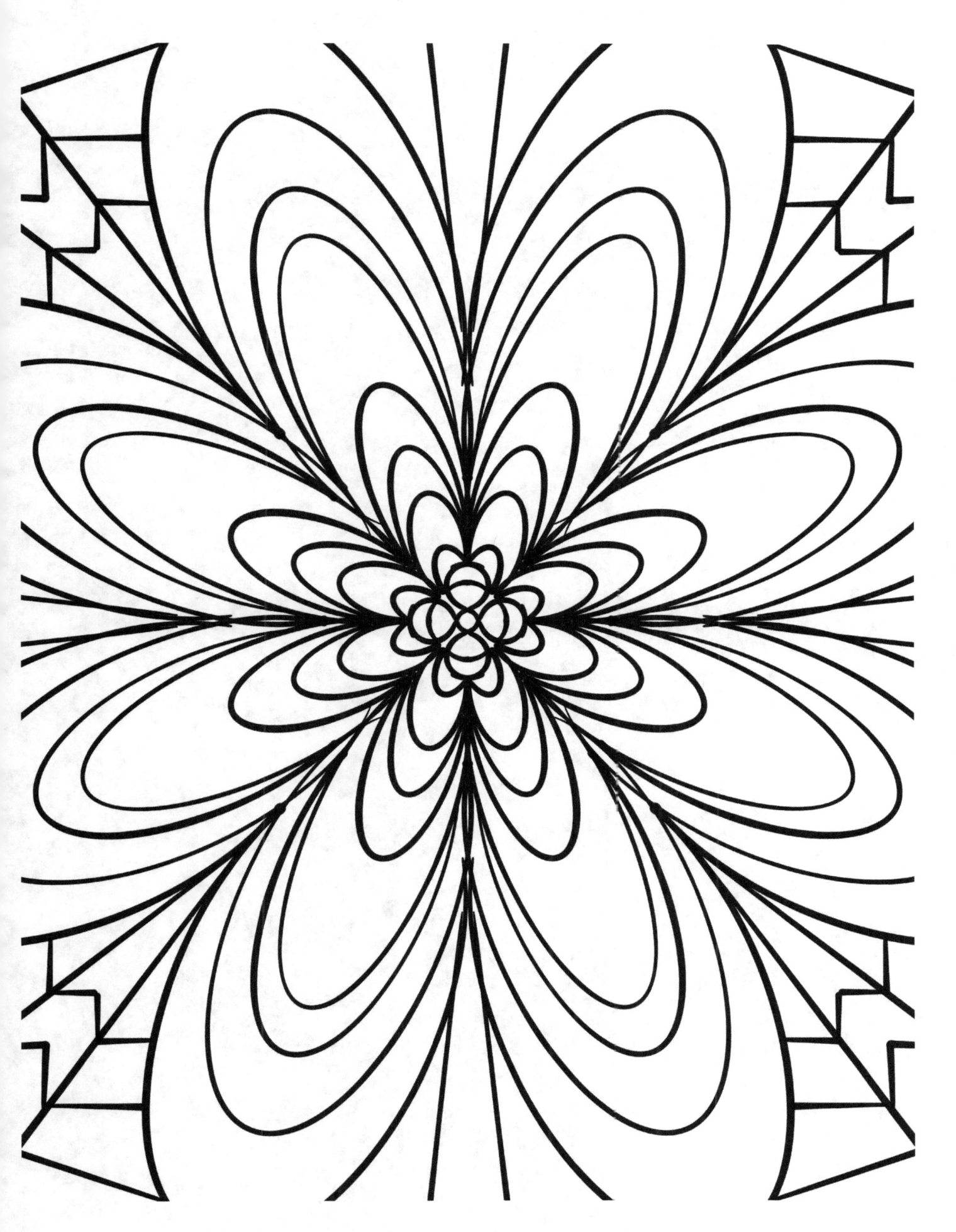

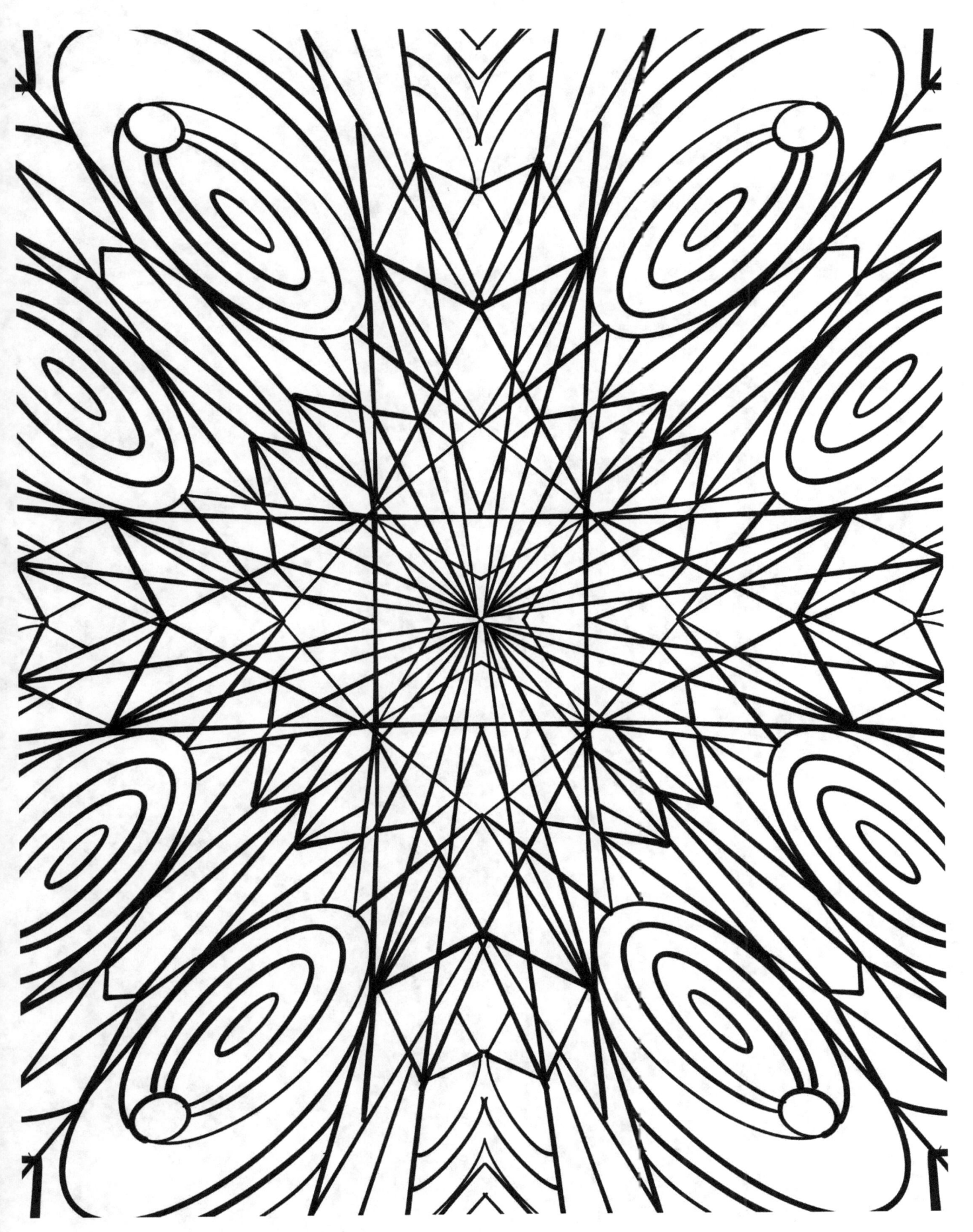

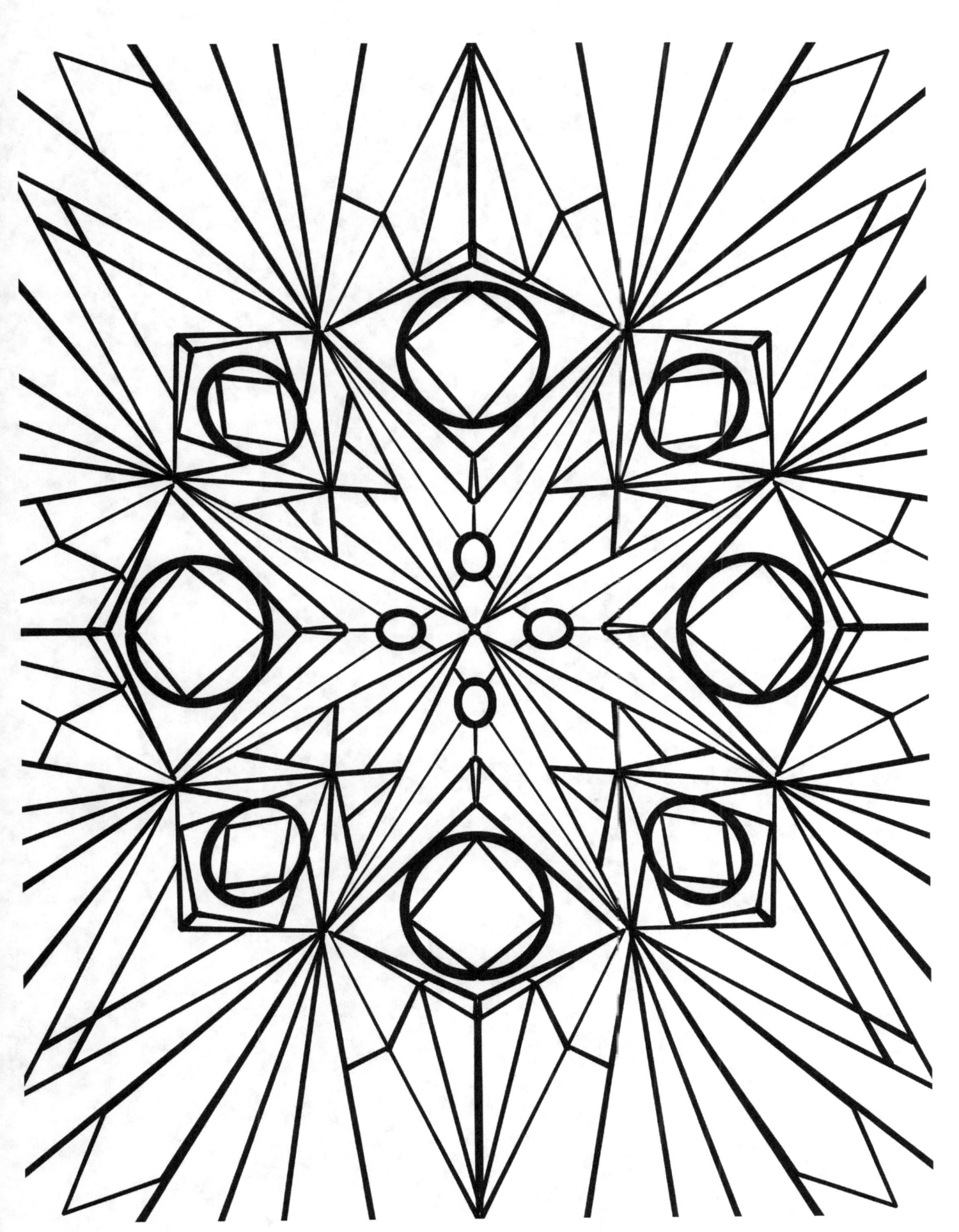

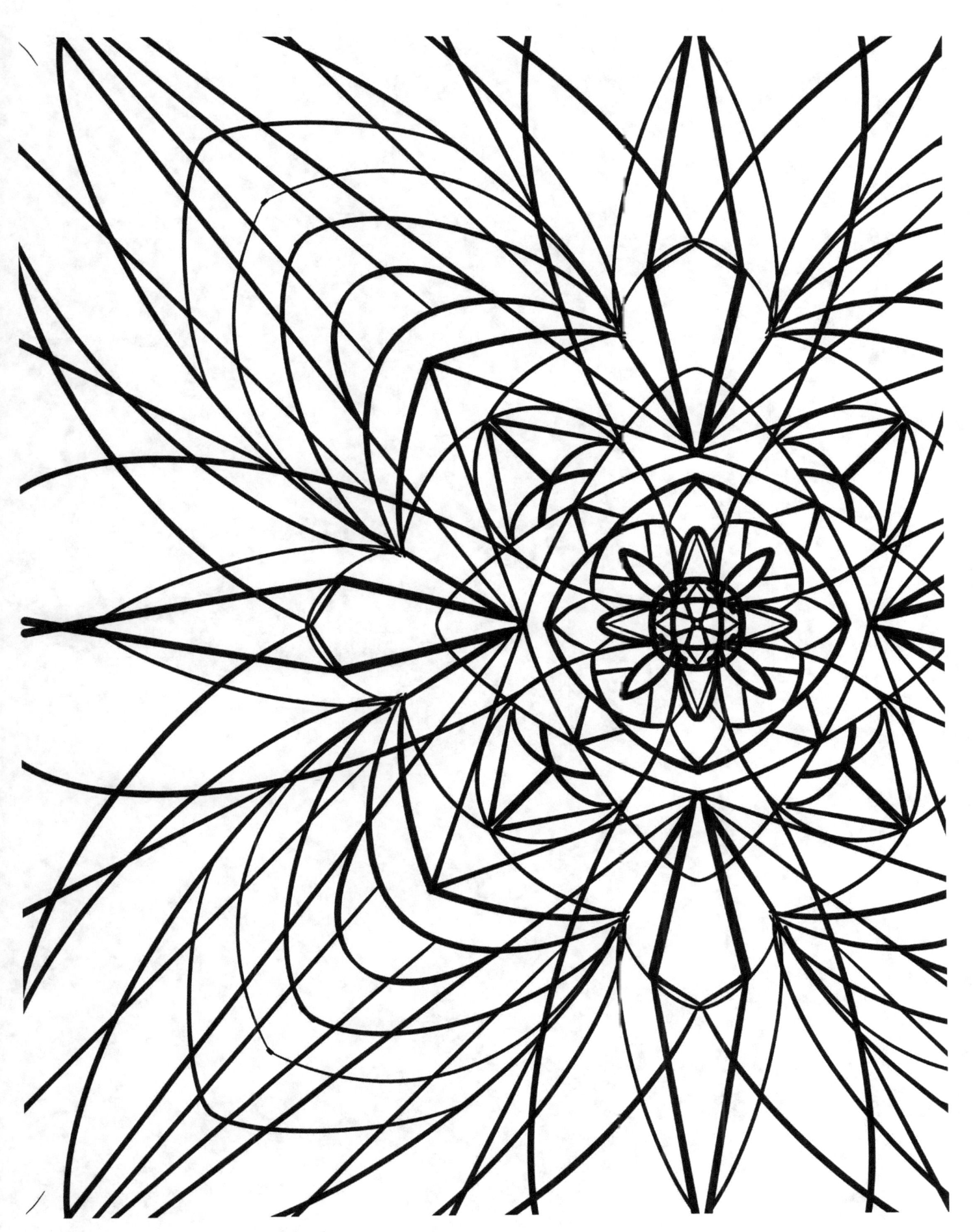

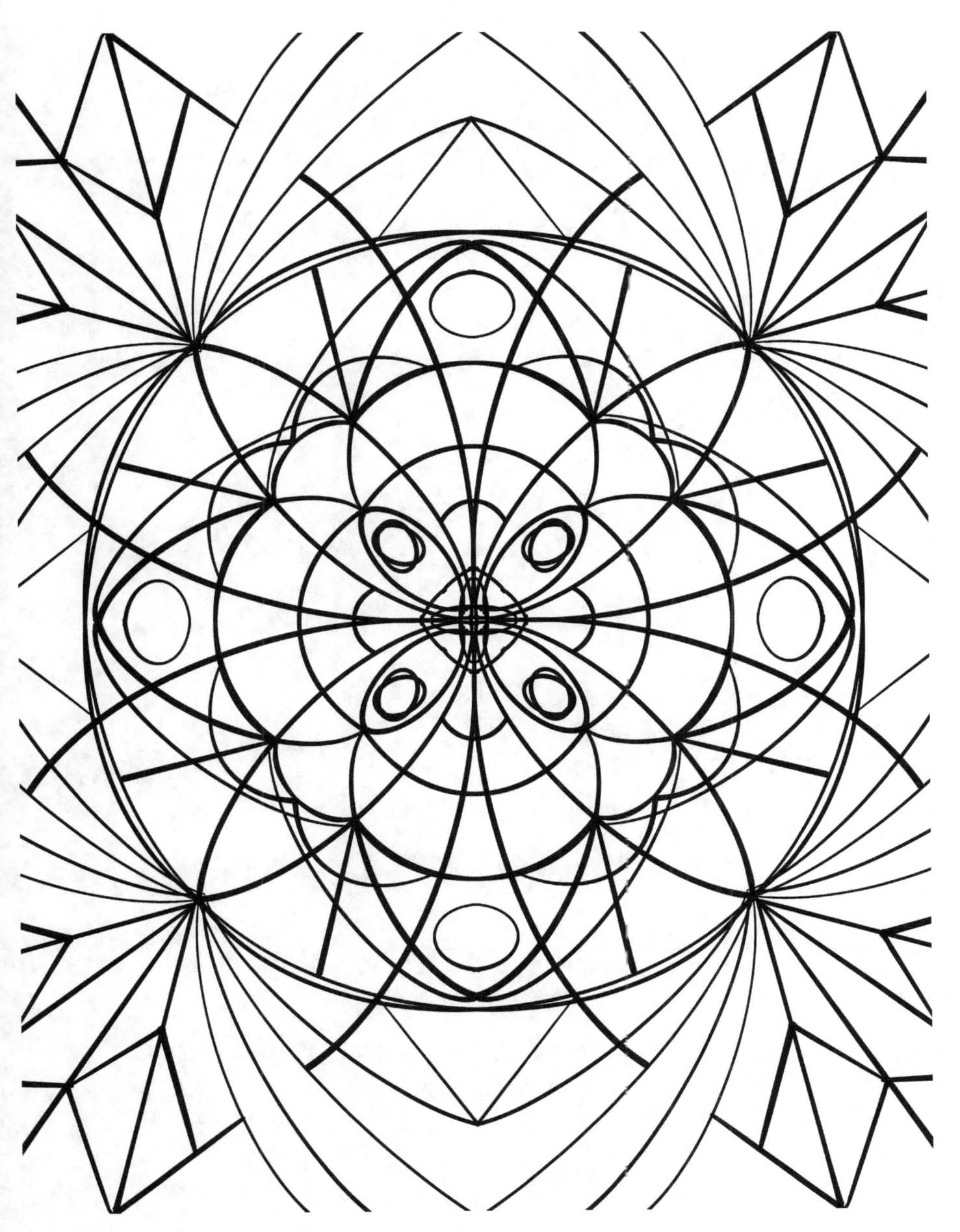

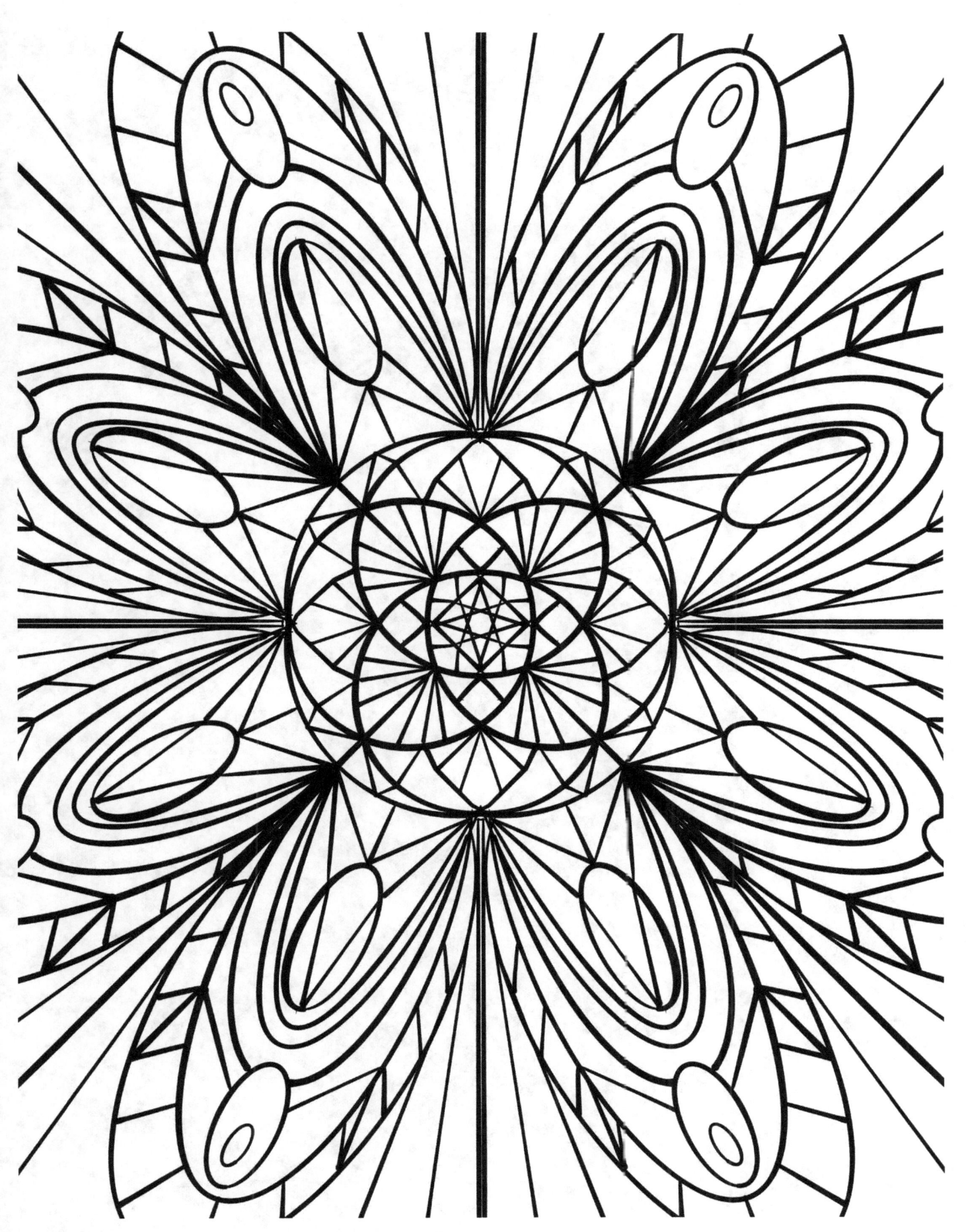

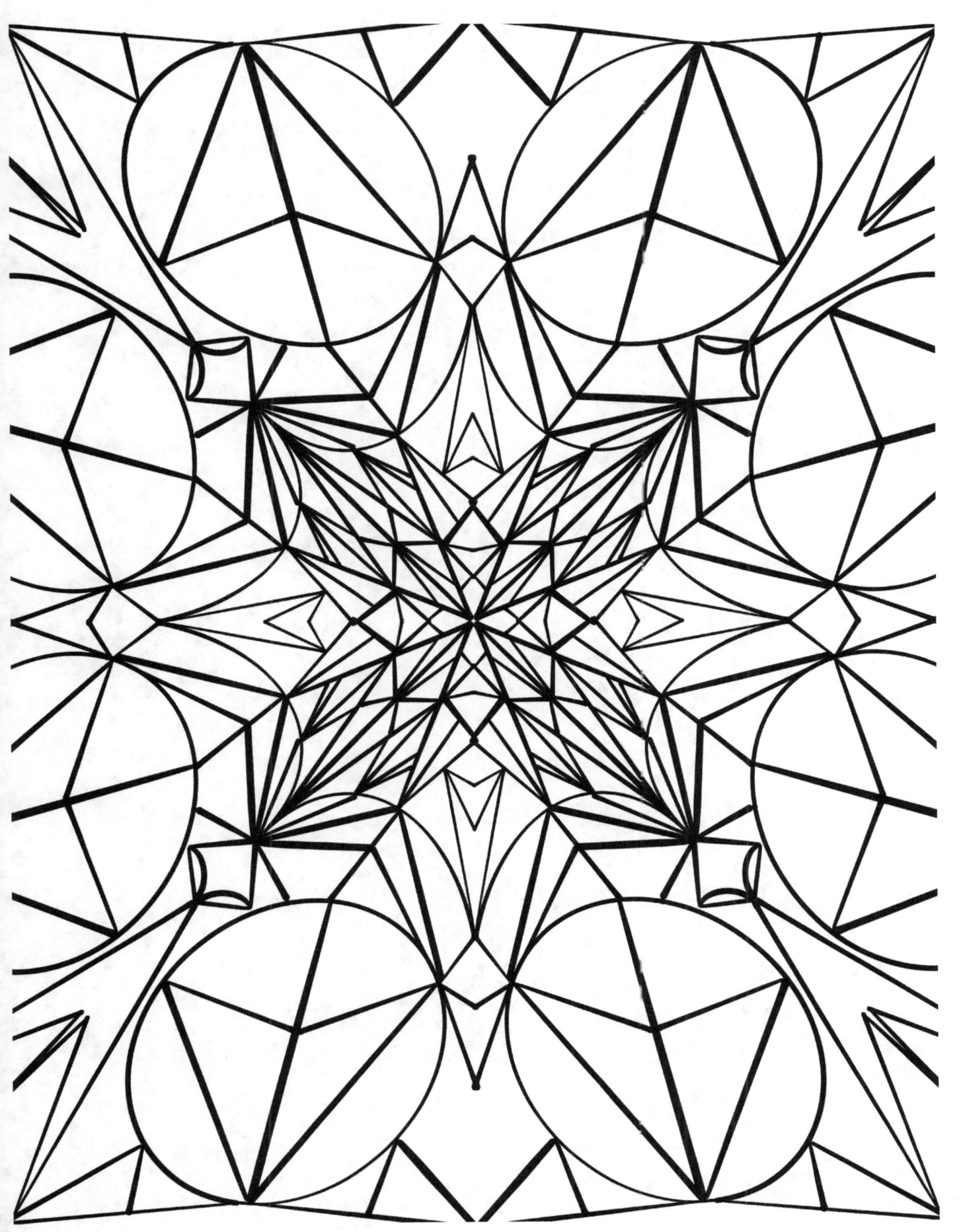

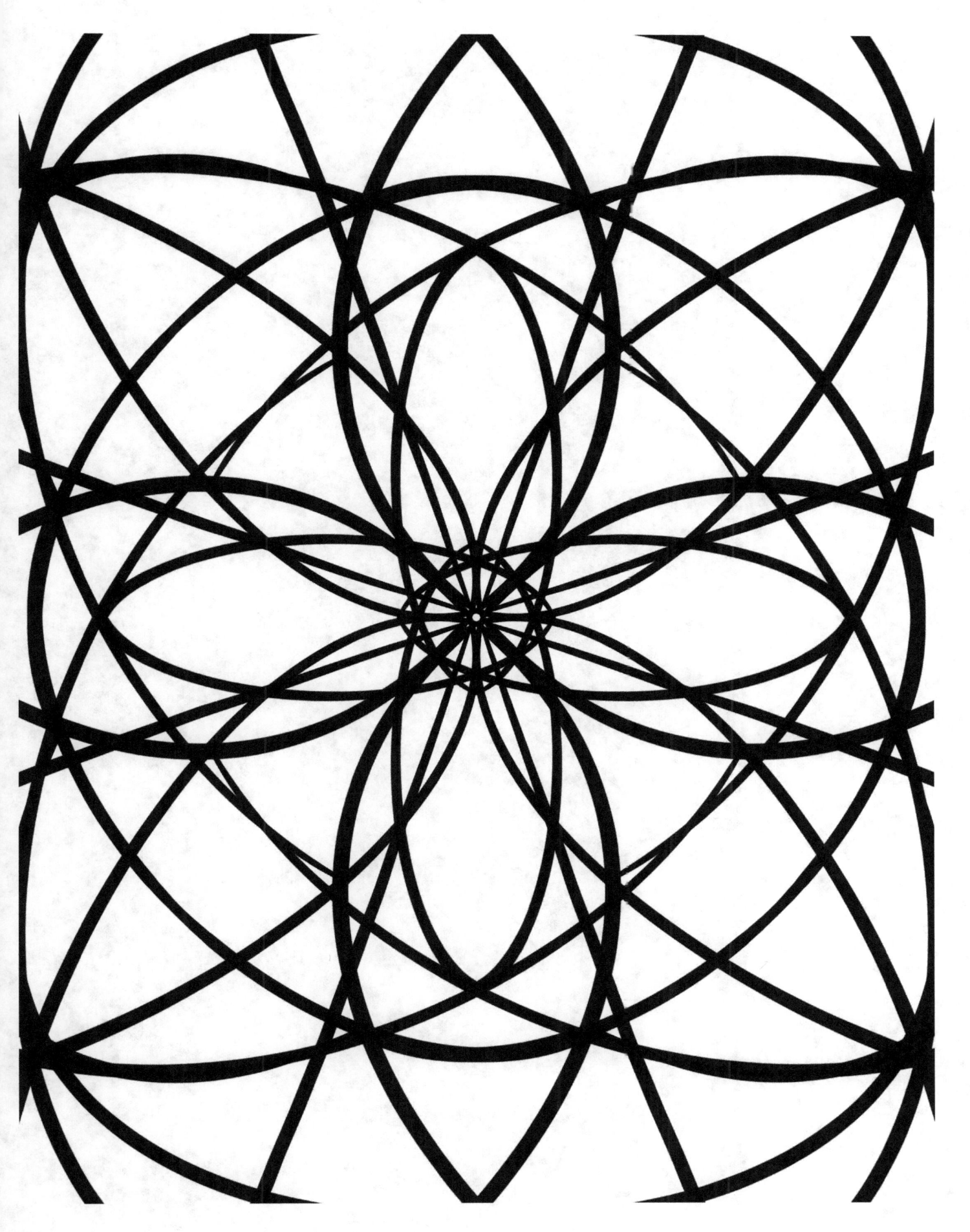

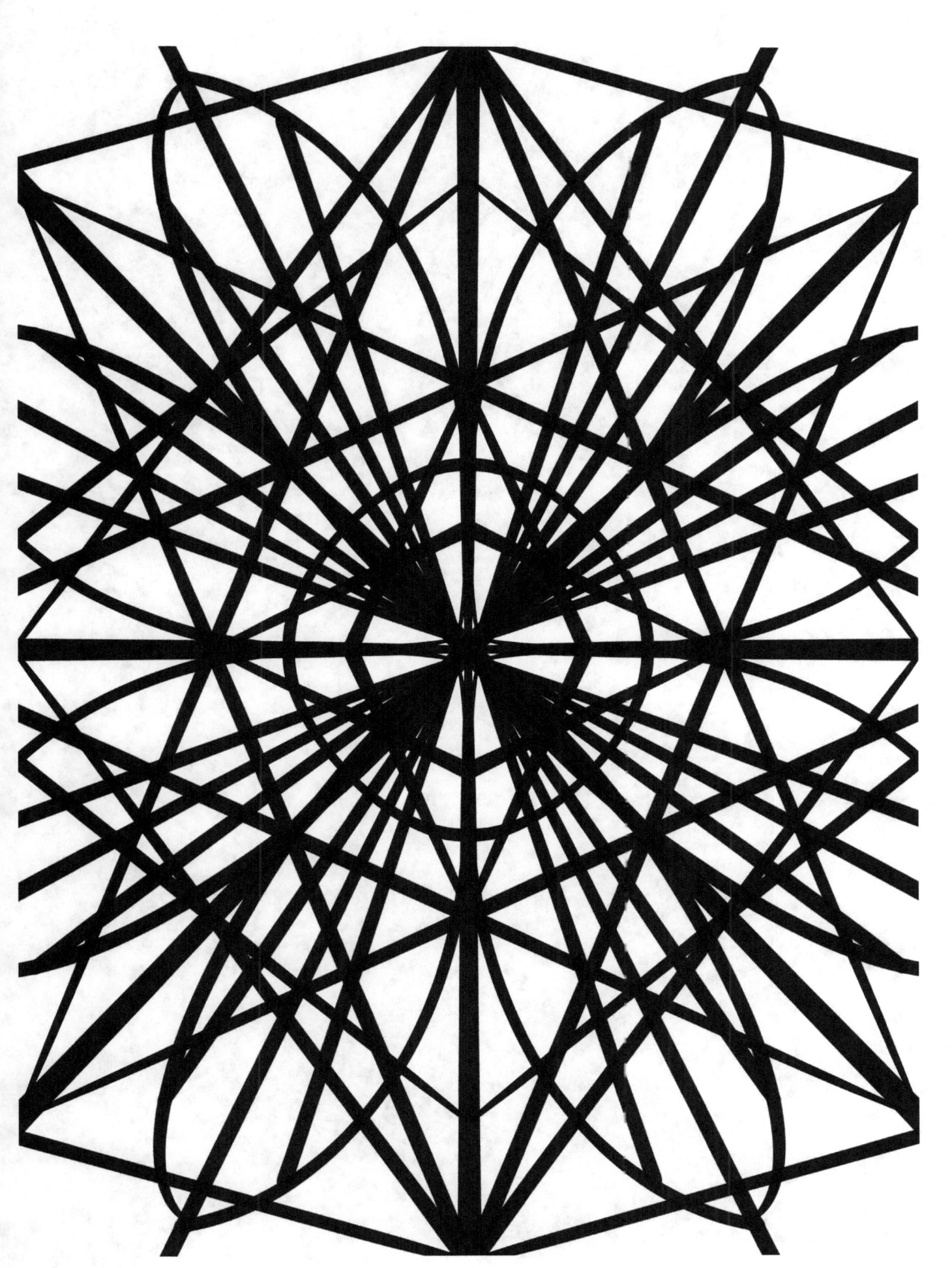

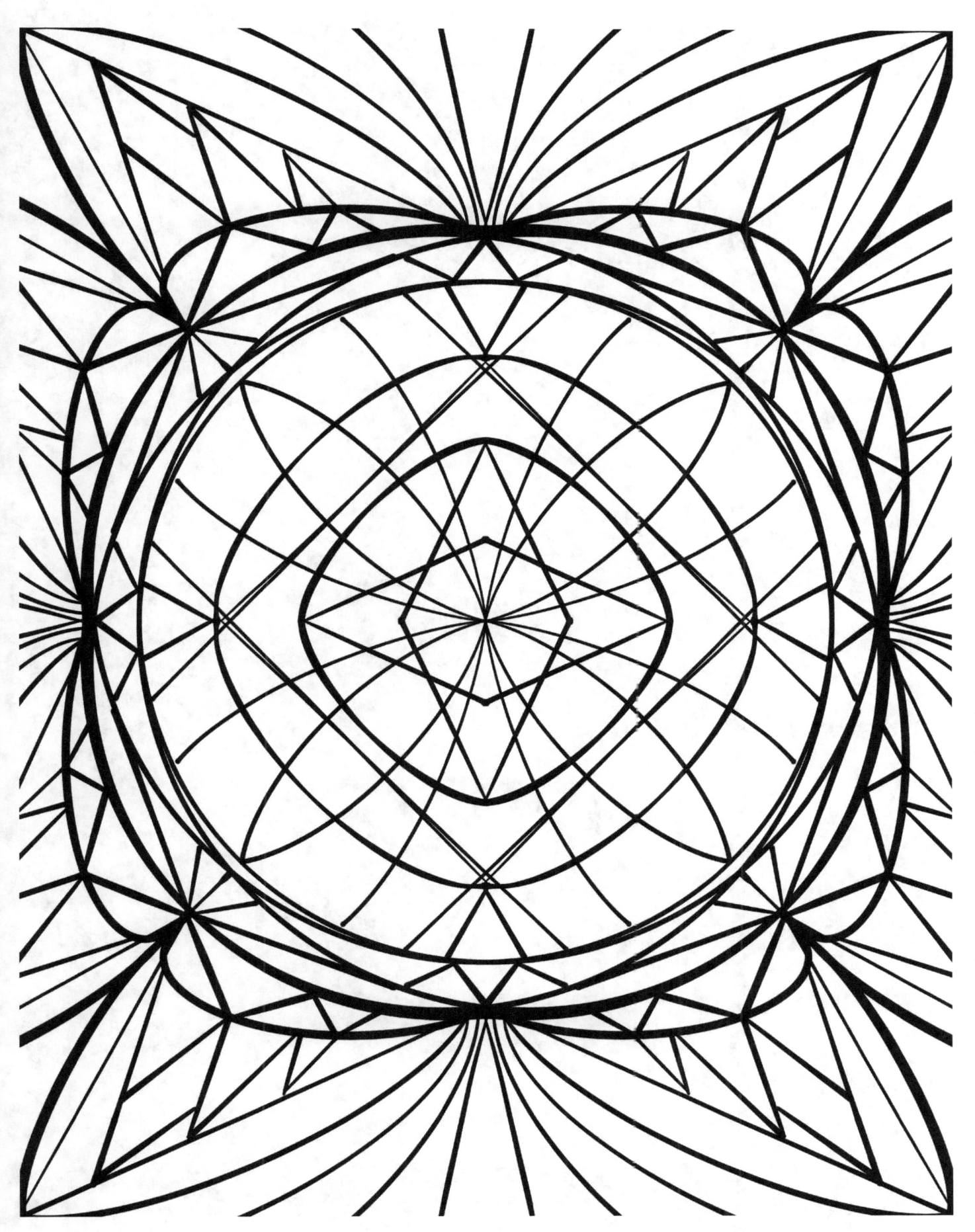

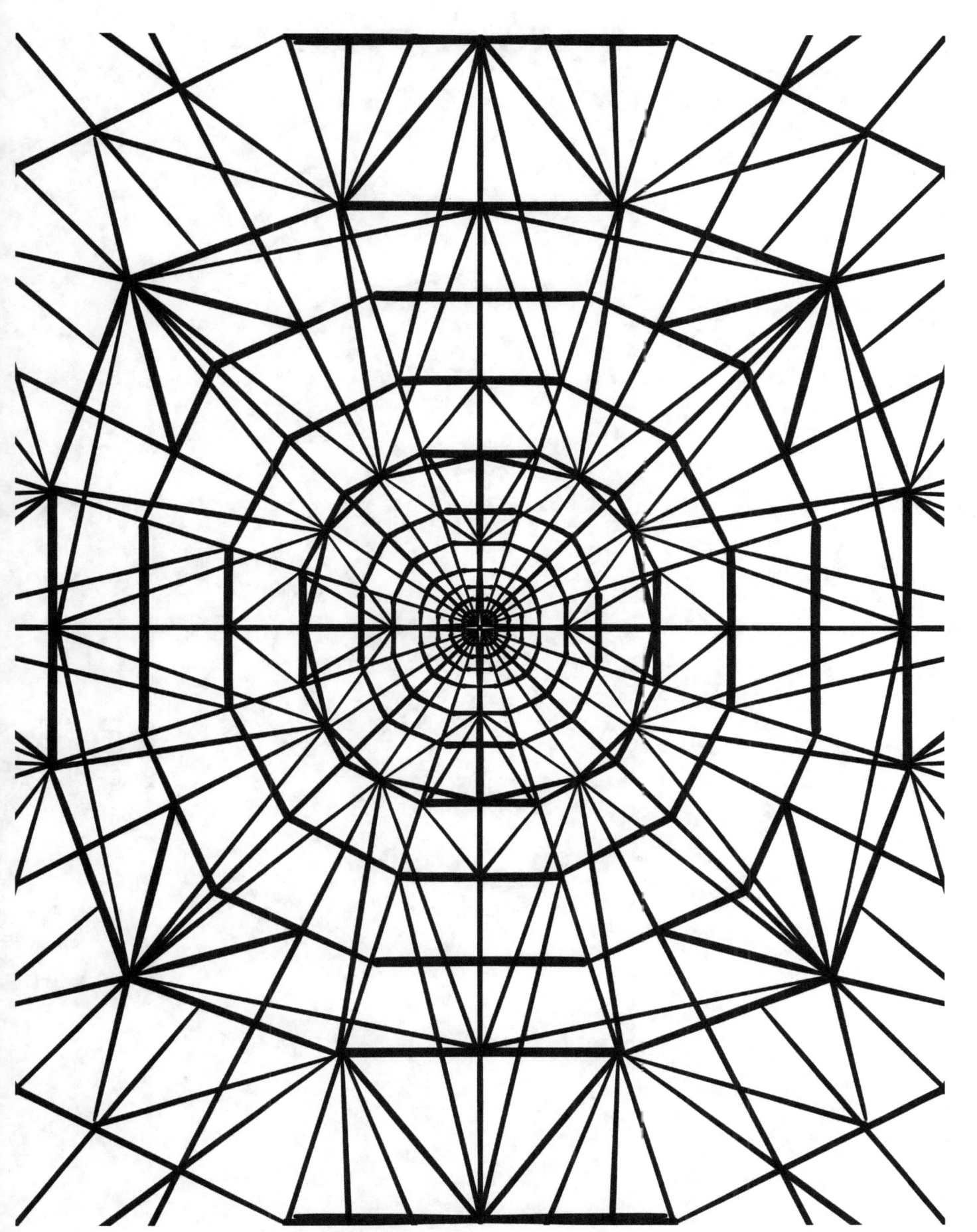

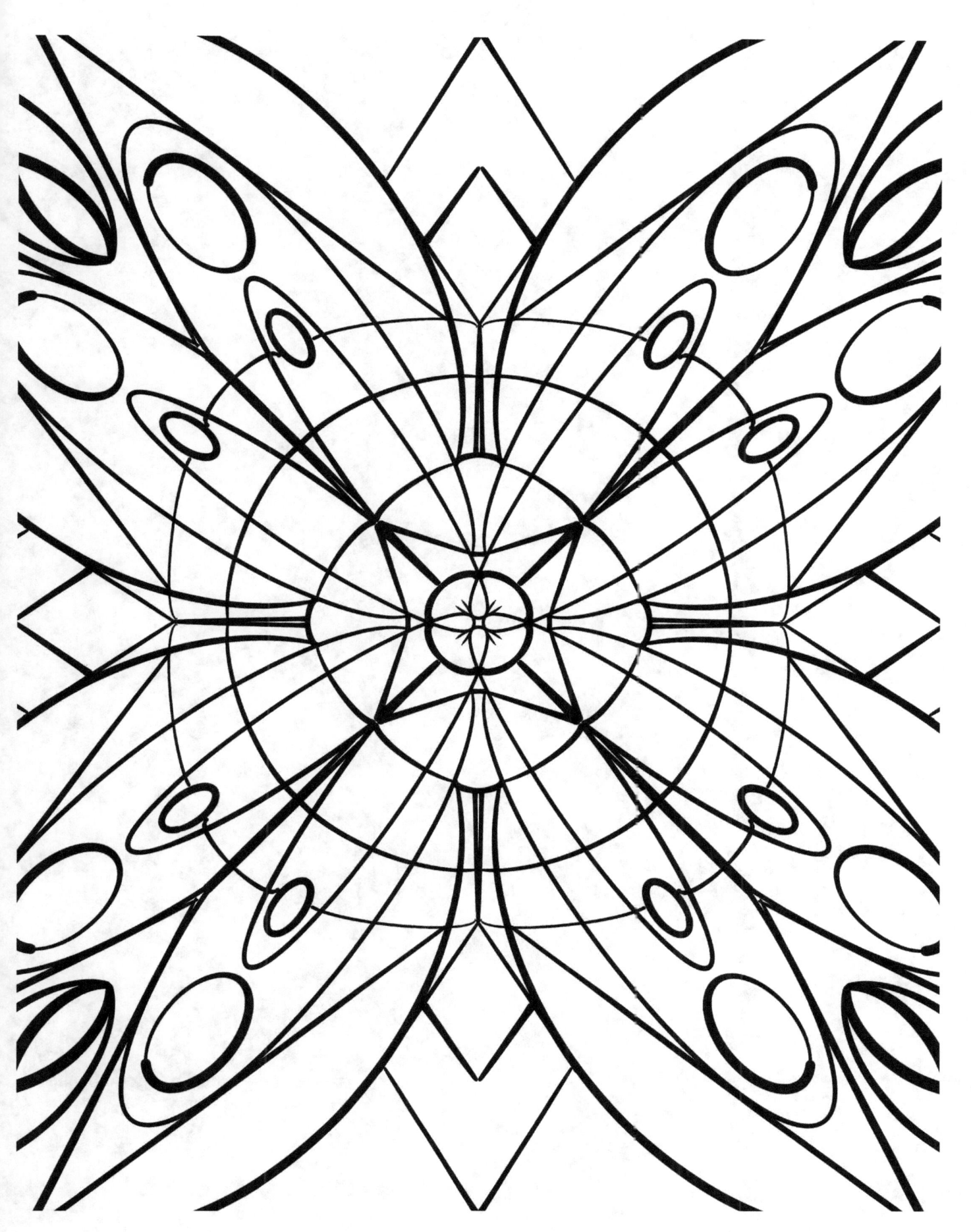

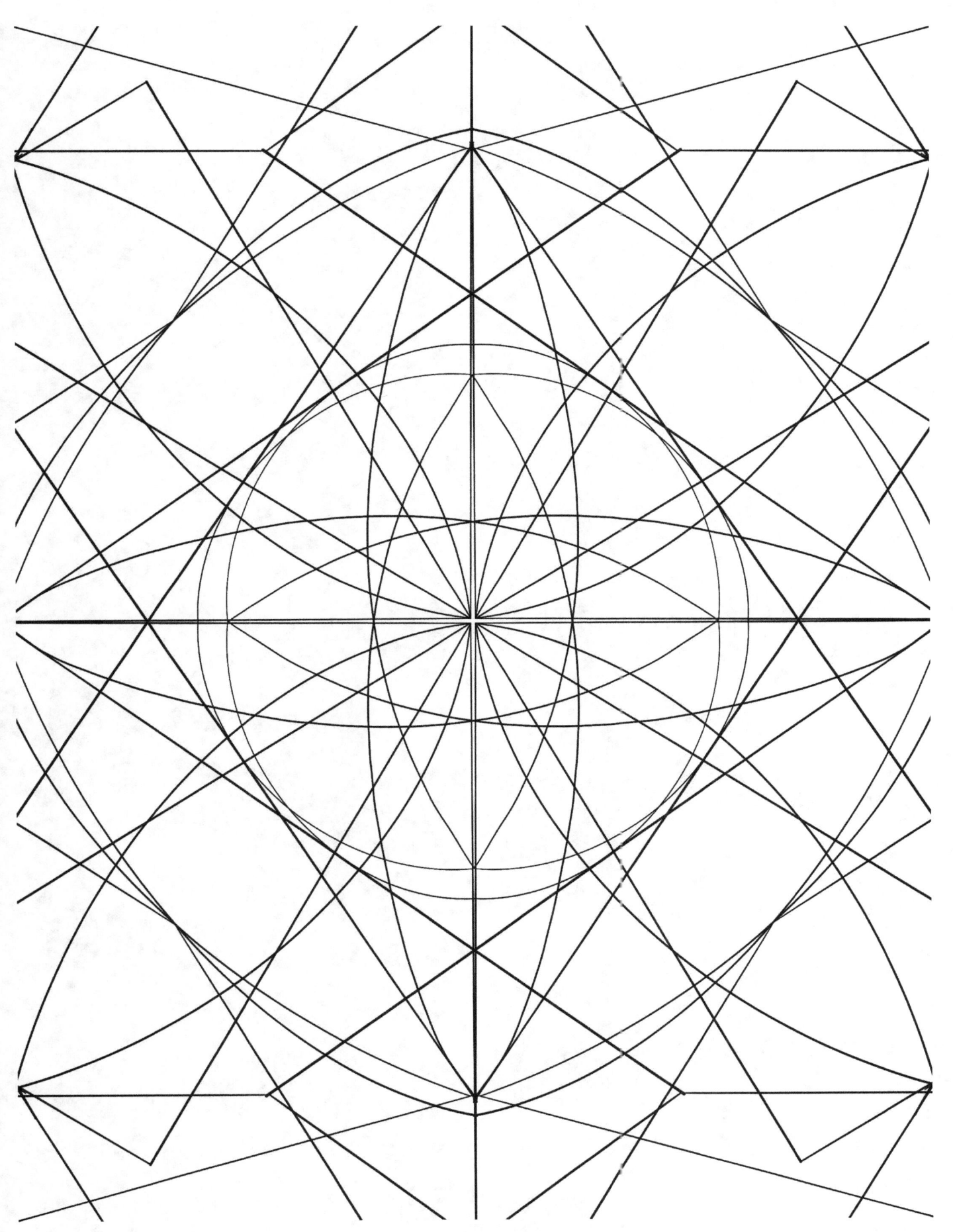

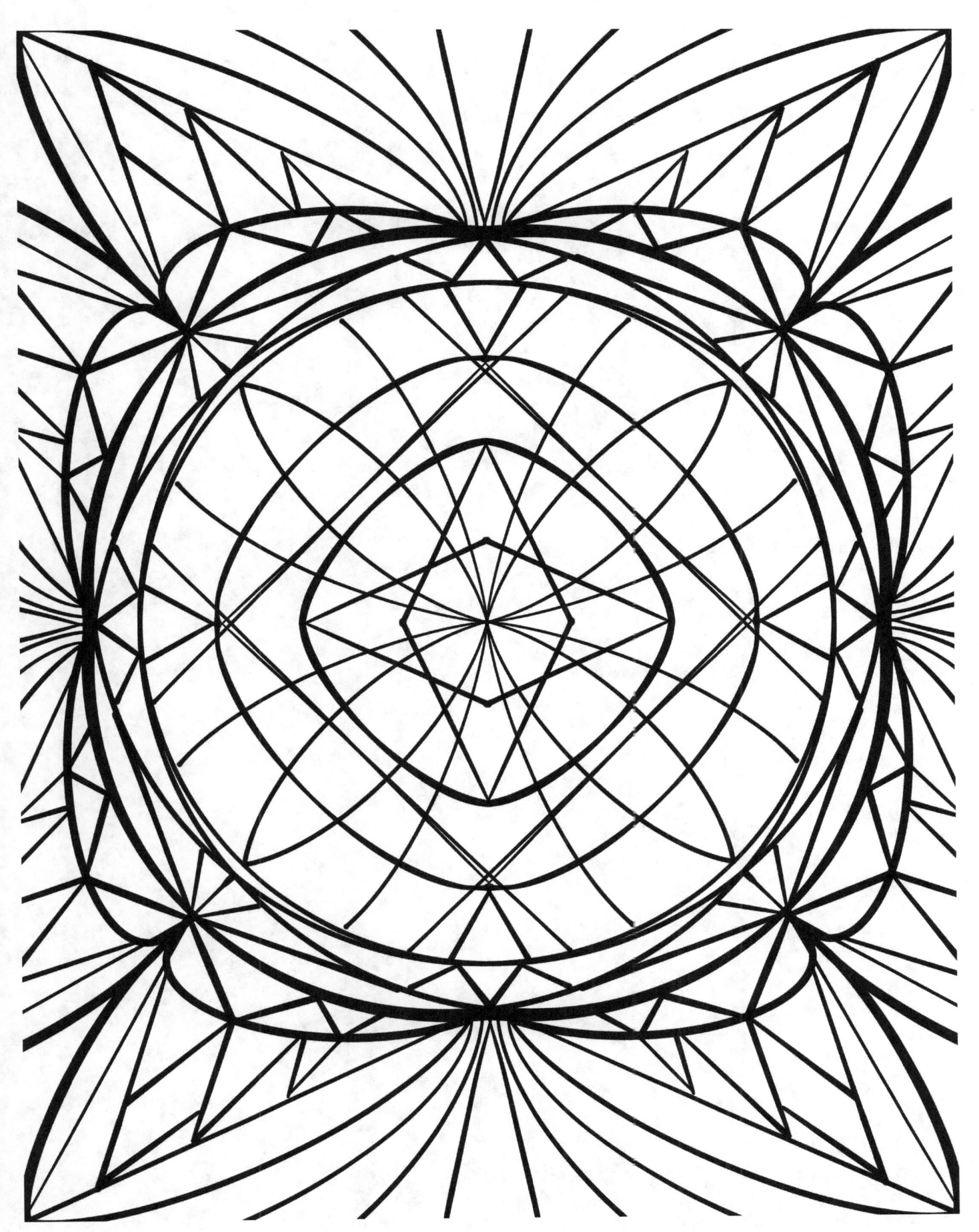

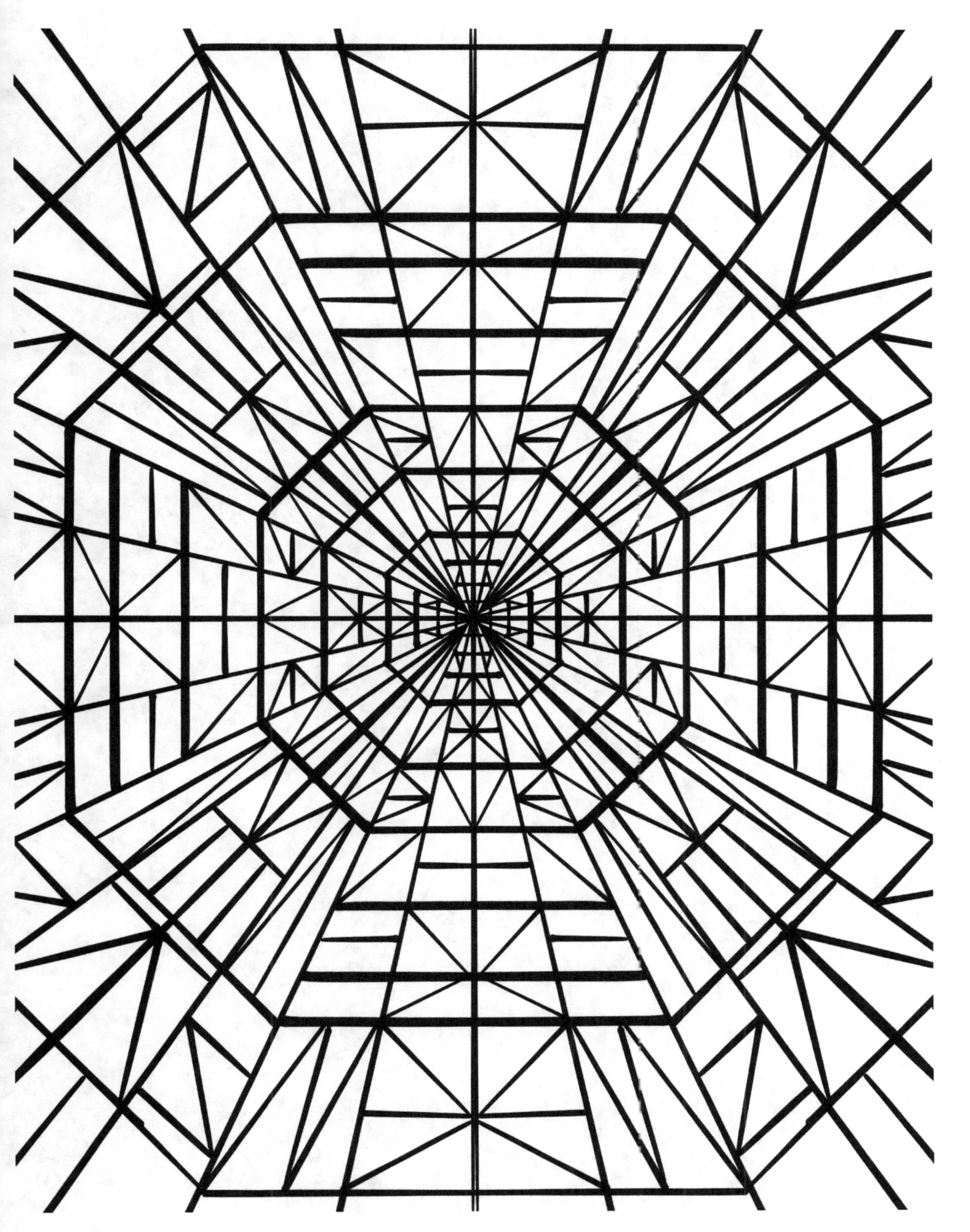

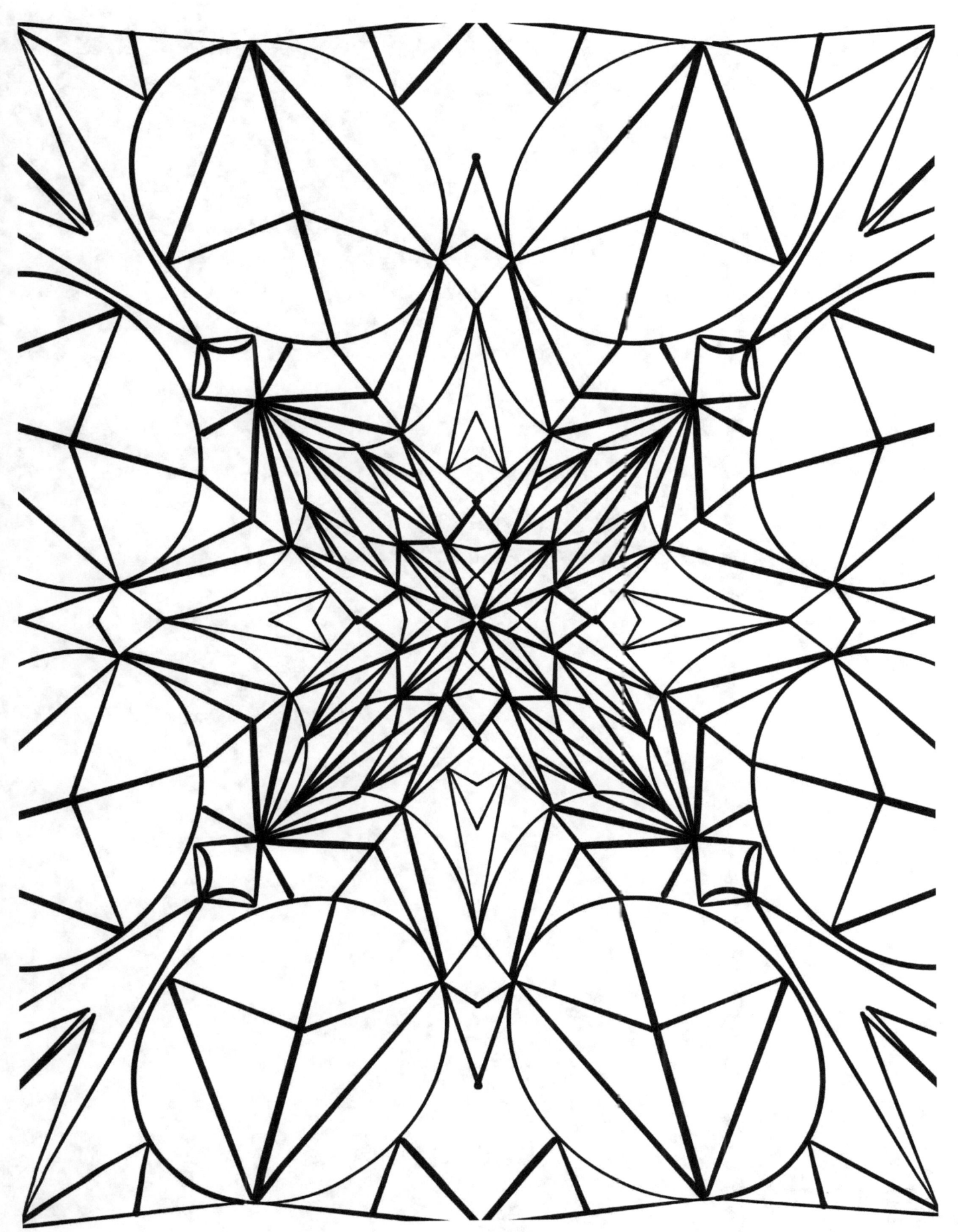

www.ingramcontent.com/pod-product-compliance
Lightning Source LLC
Chambersburg PA
CBHW060430220526
45465CB00008B/3084